NENNIUS

British History
and
The Welsh Annals

History from the Sources

NENNIUS

British History
and
The Welsh Annals

edited and translated by

JOHN MORRIS

History from the Sources
General Editor: John Morris

PHILLIMORE
London and Chichester

1980

Published by
PHILLIMORE & CO. LTD.
London and Chichester

Head Office: Shopwyke Hall,
Chichester, Sussex, England

ISBN 0 85033 297 4 (case)
ISBN 0 85033 298 2 (limp)

Printed in Great Britain

CONTENTS

INTRODUCTORY NOTE

Dr. John Morris was actively working on *Nennius* shortly before his death on 1 June 1977. The text and translation was of the *Historia Brittonum* complete and is printed here exactly as he presented it, save only for corrections and additions of an editorial nature. The Introduction was not in final form, being an outline of the general points of detail he intended to discuss and a draft of a general Introduction. In the circumstances it has seemed best to marry these two drafts rather than attempt to expand it along the lines John Morris had indicated. Although it was clearly his intention to provide a fuller annotation and critical discussion of some of the problems posed by 'Nennius', John Morris' draft notes were not in a final enough form to publish here.

The text here printed is that of L. Faral (*La Légende Arthurienne*, Vol. 3, Paris 1929) with some corrections of substance and additional passages supplied from Mommsens' edition (*Chronica Minora*, Berlin, 1892), these are enclosed with dagger symbols, thus †. . . . . .†. Square brackets enclose words not found in the text, including corrected errors as, for example, where the text mistakenly reads 'filius' for 'frater', the translation is given as [brother]. Words in italics are not found in any MSS but are supplied from the contents table prefixed to the Cambridge University MS (*L*).

Editorial additions to the Introduction are enclosed in square brackets. A text and translation of the *Annales Cambriae* has also been provided.

Bangor, May 1979   R. B. WHITE

INTRODUCTION

Nennius' SELECT DOCUMENTS (*Excerpta*) of Early British History is almost unique in ancient and medieval historical writing, both in concept and form and in originality and quality of scholarship. It passed through a series of revised editions, chiefly in the first two centuries after its first publication, whose character is veiled by the difference between modern and early medieval editorial conventions.

Modern convention marks mistakes and obscurities in the texts by the use of brackets, round, square or angular; and places editorial comment, argument and guesswork in separate notes, clearly distinguished from the text.

Medieval editors were unacquainted with brackets, and their notes took the form of 'glosses', normally incorporated in the text of later editions without indication that they were notes or glosses. The normal practice was to write a 'gloss', a comment, in the margin or between the lines of the manuscript; later copyists and editors transcribed these comments in the body of their text. They are most easily recognised in explanatory phrases beginning *id est*, or *quae est*, ('that is' or 'which is'), especially when such phrases interrupt the flow or grammatical structure of the sentence in which they occur.

The earliest full text which survives, in Harleian MS 3859, is certainly not the first edition, but is very probably the second. It already contains numerous 'glosses', and is securely dated to the year 828/9 (ch. 16). The preface, preserved only in MSS of later editions, begins 'I, Nennius, pupil of the holy Elvodug (Elfoddw), have undertaken to write down some extracts that the stupidity of the British cast out (*quae hebitudo gentis Brittanniae deiecerat*)'. The Welsh Annals (*Annales Cambriae*) record the Welsh acceptance of the Roman Easter at the instance of Elvodug (*emendante Elbodugo, homine Dei*) in 768 and his death, as Bishop of Bangor (*archiepiscopus Guenedotae*) in 809. The preface does not call him Bishop, and may have been written before his consecration, which is not known.

Other evidence determines the probable date of the first edition. A text known as the *Liber Commonei*, or *Oxoniensis Prior* (Bodleian, Auct. F.4.32), a MS of the early 9th century, dated almost certainly to

1

the year 820 (discussed, with references to earlier discussions, by Sir Ifor Williams, BBCS 7, 4, 1935, 380ff.), reproduces another work of Nennius (Nemniuus, probably for Nemnius rather than Nemnivus), rebutting the allegation of an English scholar (*scolastico Saxonici generis*) that the Welsh were illiterate, by a sharp-witted parody, concocting a joke Welsh alphabet, vaguely mocking English runes. He is said to have done so *ut . . . hebitudinem deieceret gentis suae*. The words are an adaptation of Nennius' preface, cited as a work already well-known, and strongly imply that the preface had been first published before 820, and long enough before to have become familiar to the Welsh reading public. The date of the first edition is, however, unlikely to be significantly earlier than 800. The preface contains a short bibliography, which includes 'English Annals'. The only English text extensively used is the Northern History, whose latest date is 796, the year of the accession and of the death of Offa's son; Nennius omits the genealogy of his successor Coenwulf, which is included in the extant English version of the same text (Sweet, *Oldest English Texts* p. 170, lines 100–105). The English text that Nennius used is therefore dated to 796, or very soon after. One Nennius MS date (ch. 1, 5, in MS C^2) gives a date of 806, but may of course be a corrupt figure. The incomplete Chartres MS, containing only 26 of the 66 chapters, may be a transcript from the first edition.

There is no great difference of substance between the successive editions. Each leaves out some items, and adds some new material. No mechanical rule of thumb warrants a simplistic view, that items first entered in a later edition are by definition from later sources, or are less (or more) accurate than others. All editions include bald factual statements that are amply evidenced elsewhere, as well as others that are plain and credible, but lack external confirmation, and some fanciful legends, like the Tale of Emrys, that are closer to the series of the Mabinogion than to historical narrative. The origin and external witness of each item must be examined on its own merits.

It survives in some 35 MSS, in Latin, together with a translation into Irish. No MS of the original compilation survives; all omit some material, and all add. The additions are of two kinds: glosses, or notes, of the kind which a modern editor would place at the foot of the page or end of the text, were incorporated into the body of the texts; and insertions, put in by copyists.

The principal editions are MHB, whose text is an uneven mixture of various MSS; and Mommsen in MGH, not the happiest of his products. Eleven principal MSS were selected, another 11 partially collated for some MSS. These 11 MSS are in two principal groups: Harleian and related, and Vatican and related. Mommsen relied on Huelsen to read

the Vatican MS; for Huelsen's errors, cf. Ifor Williams BBCS 11, 1943,
43. Mommsen also printed in parallel a 19th-century Latin translation
of the old Irish translation, under the name 'Nennius Interpretatus'; it
is so presented that unwary scholars have sometimes taken it for an
early medieval Latin text. Faral has also printed side by side the Harleian
and related but incomplete Chartres MS, that breaks off in the middle
of ch. 37 (at '*a me quod postulas . . .*')'

Any attempt to reconstruct Nennius' original text is uncertain and
subjective, as are conflations of the existing MSS. Here MS H is given.
Verbal differences, where other MSS say the same thing in slightly
different words, are not here given, and may be consulted in MGH, or
in the fuller critical apparatus of MHB. But all additional matter, other
than inept late medieval English glosses, is here given; either added to
the text, indicated by a separate type in the text, by daggers in the
translation; or in notes on variants. The Harleian MS also includes the
Annales Cambriae, here printed as an appendix, and Welsh genealogies,
not here given, both compositions of the school of Dyfed of the mid-
10th century; both are collated in Arthurian Sources A and GB, with
other texts of Annals and Genealogies.

It is probable that the main extant versions are contemporary with
one another; the text from which Harleian derives is dated to 829
(ch. 16), and others have slightly later dates. But L, G and related MSS
contain a note (ch. 63), apparently by Nennius himself, stating that on
the advice of his master Beulan he has left out the 'pointless' Saxon
'and other' genealogies. H and related MSS however preserve the Saxon
material, that is itself of late 8th century date (Jackson C and S). It is
likely that Nennius first issued his collection relatively early in his life;
the preface may have been written before Elvodug's death in 809, but
the popularity of the work requires more than one copy; the text dated
829 is one such; the text that omitted the Saxon genealogies is likely to
have been originally a later copy made by Nennius himself, accepting
Beulan's criticism of his first edition.

NENNIUS: CONTENTS ANALYSIS

Sections IV, V and VI offer important evidence on events. VI, the Chronographer, ends with the year 497, but the event assigned to that year has not been preserved; it was probably either the date when the text was written, or else of the Battle of Badon, fought somewhere about the mid-490s, and should be restored either 'in praesentem annum' or 'in Bellum Badonis'.

The most important text in Section IV, the Kentish Chronicle, is a rational straightforward narrative of the campaign of Vortigern and his sons against the English of Hengest and Horsa in Kent. Like the corresponding entries in the Saxon Chronicle, it relates the unsuccessful attempts of Hengest to take London. It is local to Kent, since it has nothing to say of the East Angles, whose archaeological evidence demonstrates that they were already settled in numbers at the time of Hengest's campaigns, and nothing of Vortigern himself, who was necessarily concerned with the defence of London against the East Angles as well as the men of Kent. A narrative so rational is unlikely to have been composed much later than the 6th century (any joy on distinguishing its Latin from the Latin of other sections?). An early insertion, 'qui et ipse . . . Geta', takes the ancestry of Hengest and Horsa from an English text, and adds the Welsh editor's comment, 'qui fuit . . . idolis eorum'. There is no other sign that the text owed anything to English records; and British knowledge of Kent cannot have lasted long beyond the 6th century, if so long.

The Life of Germanus is a variant of a Life whose substance was communicated by the British bishop Marcus to Heiric, before the end of the 8th century. Its substance greatly expanded the single incident of the Hallelujah victory, briefly recorded by Constantius, Germanus' contemporary biographer; the outline of the story was regarded as central to the history of Powys before the end of the 9th century, in the Pillar of Eliseg; and there is little doubt that the Life upon which it was based was composed in Britain. It gives a strong local tradition of the origin of Powys.

The Tale of Emrys is of considerable literary interest; its historical evidence shows only that stories of Ambrosius were told in north Wales in and before the 8th century. None have survived. The Life of Patrick includes an epitome of a lost 8th-century life, but adds nothing to the historical record of the 5th century.

The section on Arthur's wars is a rarity. There is ample evidence that in the 6th and 7th centuries many epics of Arthur were sung in Britain, Ireland and Brittany (see Arthurian Sources section **P** Arthur), but only two survive, the Elegy for Geraint, preserved in a modernised Middle Welsh form, perhaps of the 8th or 9th century, and the Nennius epitome. The form of the poem, listing battles in separate verses, is Irish; and similar songs were sung of Arthur's great Irish contemporary, Mac Erc. The location of some of the few identifiable sites, in the north and west, argues that not all the campaigns were fought against the English, or Saxons, though Nennius assumed that they were. It indicates that, before Badon, the campaign that was regarded as most important was fought in Lincolnshire; its location presupposes previous successful campaigns against the East and Middle Angles, cf. *Age of Arthur*, p. 82.

Section V, the 6th and 7th centuries, slots together a number of different English and British traditions about the north; and between the pedigrees of the Bernicians and the Deiras interposes genealogies of the Mercians and the Kentish, but not of the West Saxons. These pedigrees are taken to the end of the 8th century; but they stop before the accession of Egbert and the formation of the Wessex genealogical tradition. The historical narrative is however taken only to the later 7th century, and ends with the death of Egferth in 685, when the Northumbrians ceased from wars. Parts of the British narrative, notably the word, *Atbret*, are earlier rather than later than Egferth's time.

The composition of this section has been fully discussed by K. H. Jackson in *Celt and Saxon*. Apart from its genealogies, it forms a continuous narrative, synchronising Northumbrian, British and Mercian tradition. It begins with Ida, and equates him with British notices of Outigirn and Maelgwn, in the middle-6th century. Next follows Ida's sons, equated with Urien and his sons and contemporaries. Edwin and Oswald are then equated with Catwallaun, Oswy with Penda and

Catgabail. After a sentence, a paragraph summarises Penda of Mercia, and gives the British name of the Battle of Cogwy. There is no mention of Wulfhere, 658 onward, or later Mercian kings. It is possible that this section was drawn up in Aldfrith's reign, about the 690s, and the genealogies added a century later.

[On 'Some Aspects of the Chronology of the *Historia Brittonum*' see D. N. Dumville, *B.B.C.S.* 25 (1972–4), 439–445, where the 'Chronographer' (caps. 16 and 66) is examined, Dumville calculates a date of *c.*829–830 for 4 Merfyn Frych, perhaps also giving the date of compilation of the *Historia*. The 'Chronographer' (cap. 66) had access to the consular dates (which he obviously understood) given in the *Cursus Pascalis* of Victorius (Mommsen, *Chronica Minora*, Vol. I, Berlin 1892).

RBW]

Parts of the Northern History show knowledge of the matter that Bede relates; but there is nothing to show that it used Bede; it is more likely to have been among Bede's sources.

The last two sections, the Cities and the Wonders, are both named by Nennius as pre-existing works that he transcribed, probably early in the 9th century. Both are composite documents; the Wonders is centred on Gwent, but consists of a conflation of several different versions of the same stories, by an author who was not personally familiar with Gwent. The remarkable phenomenon of the Severn Bore is told several times over, with variant names, the author being unaware that they were the same phenomenen.

The principal interest of the earlier sections is their illustration of the level of knowledge, and of the attitudes of scholars in north Wales about the year 800. It is a single and invaluable guide to learning, letters and Latinity in an age and region of which virtually nothing else is known.

The historical concept of Nennius' compilation is original, and startlingly modern. Almost all ancient, medieval, and early modern historians undertook narrative histories giving their own interpretation of their sources, or else compiled annalistic chronicles of events. Nennius did not. In his words, he 'made a heap of all he found'. He copied the documents he found, of very different quality and kind, not continuously. He selected extracts from each source, and arranged them usually in what he thought was their proper chronological order, sometimes grouped by subject matter; and in his preface he listed an outline bibliography of his main sources. This is the technique of the modern selective source book, used, for example, by Lewis and Rheinhold and

6

by A. H. M. Jones for ancient history, and by Gardener, Douglas and many others for medieval and modern history.

Nennius' intensive search for exact dates, and his attempts to link documentary with material evidence, also anticipate modern techniques, though the differences between the resources available to scholars of the early 9th and the late-20th centuries easily obscure the scale of his undertaking and the application he concentrated upon it. The modern scholar is equipped with twelve centuries of simple straightforward dating, running from a fixed starting year, A.D. 1, to the present day; and the researches of his recent predecessors have long since attached secure A.D. dates to ancient events described by other dating systems. When Nennius worked, A.D. dating, pioneered in its modern form by Bede's History, was only just beginning to win wide acceptance. It was altogether unknown to the writers whose works he excerpted; and continued to bedevil Irish and Welsh annalistic tradition for centuries to come. Nennius' numerous and involved computations of date appear cumbersome, sometimes baffling and irritating, to the modern reader. Nennius' endeavour to fit A.D. dates to older texts which knew them not was a prodigious undertaking. Comparable work on the main body of European Chronicles of late antiquity and the early middle ages was not satisfactorily concluded until the 19th century; and a good many datings assigned to late Roman events by 18th-century scholars are wider of the mark than Nennius' reckonings of British events undertaken a thousand years earlier.

Nennius' occasional use of material evidence, especially inscriptions, is also original in his day and age. The most striking instance is his note to the short account of Claudius' conquest of Britain. 'His monument is to be seen at Moganza in Lombardy (*in Mogantia apud Longobardos*); he died there on his way back to Rome.' The basis of this note is the monument to the emperor's uncle, Tiberius Claudius Drusus, at Moguntiacum (Mainz) in the Rhineland (C.I.L. XIII). Nennius had seen or heard of a copy or abstract of the inscription; he identified the wrong Claudius, and muddled Mogantia with Moguntiacum. Mistakes of this order are still commonplace in the developed modern discipline of epigraphy, the study of inscriptions. The relevant academic journals abound with articles demonstrating that this or that person has been wrongly identified with someone else of the same name; and the British volume of the modern *Corpus* of Latin Inscriptions, compiled by a 19th-century Berlin scholar, confused Derbyshire with Denbighshire. Occasional publications set forth errors far more absurd than Nennius; the inscription of a 2nd-century Roman senator, beginning with the name *C(aio) Cilnio*, with letters ligatured, joined together, was first published as *C(aio) C(ai) l(iberto) No(cturno)*, 'to Caius Nocturnus,

7

freedman of Caius', a few decades ago. The inference that Claudius was buried in Lombardy because he died there on his way back from Britain, made in the absence of available evidence that Claudius lived 10 years more, is comparable with inferences drawn by many modern scholars in the absence of contrary evidence. Nennius' error is also somewhat less drastic than the one other known use of epigraphic evidence by an early British historian. Bede, copying the genealogy of the Kings of Kent, noted that the monument of Hengest's legendary brother Horsa might be seen in Kent, reading HORS. The stone reported to Bede was evidently a fragment of an inscription erected by a /co/HORS, an army cohort, or battalion, since Kent is the only part of south-eastern Britain where a cohort was garrisoned, the I Baetasiorum at Reculver from the early 3rd century, at times when stone inscriptions were normally erected.

It does not behove the well-equipped modern scholar to smile at the scholarship which Nennius applied to his limited resources. He judged soundly in rejecting the contemporary fashions of historical writing. His contemporaries either compiled Annals, juggling with entries in contradictory order in their sources, without trying to seek absolute dates from external sources; or else wrote narrative histories, selecting and highlighting incidents that fitted their purpose and viewpoint, with critical judgement confined to the morality and intentions of persons, their main objective to edify by elegant presentation. Nennius knew Bede's dating; he may or may not have known his History; but he knew that he had not the material with which to compose a comparable history of the Welsh. In deciding to publish extracts and abridgements of his sources rather than a history, supplied with such editorial notes as he was able to provide, he accepted a modest target, within the limits of the knowledge at his disposal. His decision was original, without precedent, and for long without sequel. It gave to posterity an insight into the history of Britain between the Romans and the English that, for all its patchiness, was clearer than any narrative history written in early 9th-century Wales could have achieved. At the same time he pioneered a new historical method, a tool of historical research that could not be adequately exploited until our own day, and has not yet reached its full development.

12 November 1975   JOHN MORRIS

†HISTORY OF THE BRITISH†

† assembled by †

† the learned Nennius †

† Extracts found by [Rhun] son of Urien in the Book of
Saint Germanus on the origin and descent of the British †

† PREFACE †

† I, Nennius, pupil of the holy Elvodug, have undertaken to write down some
extracts that the stupidity of the British cast out; for the scholars of the
island of Britain had no skill, and set down no record in books. I have therefore made a heap of all that I have found, both from the Annals of the
Romans and from the Chronicles of the Holy Fathers, and from the writings
of the Irish and the English, and out of the tradition of our elders.

Many learned scholars and copyists have tried to write, but somehow
they have left the subject more obscure, whether through repeated pest-
ilence or frequent military disasters. I ask every reader who reads this
book to pardon me for daring to write so much here after so many, like a
chattering bird or an incompetent judge. I yield to whoever may be better
acquainted with this skill than I am. †

† CONTENTS †

† The Ages of the World †

9

10

[Roman Britain]

[After the Roman Dominion]

[THE KENTISH CHRONICLE, PART 1]

[THE LIFE OF SAINT GERMANUS, PART 1]

13

[THE CAMPAIGNS OF ARTHUR]

[NORTHERN HISTORY]

15

lxvi 67 The great lake Lummonou, which is called Loch Leven in English, in the land of the Picts, and of the 340 islands in it, inhabited by men; and of the same number of rocks around it, and of the 340 eagles' nests placed on them; and of as many rivers that flow into the lake, and that only one river, which is called the Leven, flows to the sea.

lxvii 67 The river that rises up like a high mountain.

lxviii 67 The Hot Lake, in which are the Baths of Badon, agreeable to the desire of each man's wish.

lxix 68 The salted springs, from which boiled water is turned into salt.

lxx 68 How the foaming waters on the Severn shore build up, withdraw, advance and fight each other.

lxxi 69 How lake Lliwan devours and spews up, swells and consumes, and turns unwilling horsemen around, and drags them to itself.

lxxii 70 The spring of Gorheli, in which four kinds of fish are found.

lxxiii 70 The ash-tree that bears apples, by the river Wye.

lxxiv 70 The wind that issues from a pit in the land of Gwent.

lxxv 71 The altar of Llwynarth that stands on nothing, but is suspended by the will of God, and of the body of a saint buried by the altar, and of the swift punishment which two men received because of it.

lxxvi 72 The spring by the wall of Meurig's Well, and of the wood found in it, how it stays three days in the sea and is always found there again on the fourth day.

lxvii 73 The footprint of Cabal, Arthur's hound, in the land of Builth; and of the stone placed on the pile of rocks, how it is often taken away, but is always still to be found there.

lxxviii 73 The tomb of Amr, which has often been measured, but will never be found to measure the same.

The Wonders of the Island of Mona,
called in English Anglesey,
that is, the Island of the English

The Wonders of Ireland

End of the Contents †

[THE SIX AGES OF THE WORLD]

1. From the Beginning of the World to the Flood are 2,242 years. From the Flood to Abraham are 942 years. From Abraham to Moses are 640 years. From Moses to David are 500 years.

2. From David to Nebuchadnezzar are 569 years. From Adam to the Babylonian Migration are 4,879 years.

3. From the Babylonian Migration to Christ are 566 years. From Adam therefore to the Passion of Christ are 5,228 years.

4. From the Passion of Christ 796 years have passed; from the Incarnation 831 years.

5. The First Age of the World is therefore from Adam to Noah. The Second Age is from Noah to Abraham, the Third Age from Abraham to David.

6. The Fourth Age is from David to Daniel, the Fifth Age from Daniel to John the Baptist, the Sixth Age from John to the Judgement, when Our Lord Jesus Christ will come to judge the living and the dead and the world through fire.

[BRITISH AND IRISH ORIGINS]

7. The island of Britain is so called from one Brutus, a Roman consul. It reaches from the south-west northward, and lies to the west. It is 800 miles long, 200 broad. In it are twenty-eight cities and head-lands without number, together with innumerable forts built of stone and brick, and in it live four nations, the Irish, the Picts, the Saxons and the British.

8. It has three large islands. One of them lies towards Armorica, and is called the Isle of Wight; the second is situated in the middle of the sea between Ireland and Britain, and is named Eubonia, that is Man; the other is situated at the extreme edge of the world of Britain, beyond the Picts, and is called Orkney. So the old saying runs, when rulers and kings are mentioned, 'He ruled Britain with its three islands'.

9. In Britain there are many rivers, that flow in all directions, to the east, west, south and north. But two of the rivers excel beyond the rest, the Thames and Severn, like the two arms of Britain, on which

ships once travelled, carrying goods for the sake of commerce. The British once occupied and ruled it all from sea to sea.

10. If anyone wants to know when this island was inhabited after the Flood, I find two alternative explanations. The version in the Annals of the Romans is that after the Trojan War Aeneas came to Italy with his son Ascanius, defeated Turnus and married Lavinia, daughter of Latinus, son of Faunus, son of Picus, son of Saturn; and after Latinus' death, he acquired the kingdom of the Romans and the Latins. Aeneas founded Alba, and then married a wife, who bore him a son named Silvius. Silvius married a wife, who became pregnant, and when Aeneas was told that his daughter-in-law was pregnant, he sent word to his son Ascanius, to send a wizard to examine the wife, to discover what she had in the womb, whether it was male or female. The wizard examined the wife and returned, but he was killed by Ascanius because of his prophecy, for he told him that the woman had a male in her womb, who would be the child of death, for he would kill his father and his mother, and be hateful to all men. So it happened; for his mother died in his birth, and the boy was reared, and named Britto. Much later, according to the wizard's prophecy, when he was playing with others, he killed his father with an arrow shot, not on purpose, but by accident. He was driven from Italy, and came to the islands of the Tyrrhene Sea, and was driven from Greece, because of the killing of Turnus, whom Aeneas had killed, and arrived in Gaul, where he founded the city of Tours, which is called Turnis; and later he came to this island, which is named Britannia from his name, and filled it with his race, and dwelt there. From that day, Britain has been inhabited until the present day.

† This is the genealogy of that Brutus the Hateful, who has never been traced to us, when the Irish, who do not know their (?) origin, wished to be under him (?), † This is how our noble elder Cuanu gathered the genealogy of the British from the chronicles of the Romans.†
Brutus was the son of Silvius, son of Ascanius, son of Aeneas, son of Anchises, son of Capen, son of Asaracus, son of Tros, son of Erectonius, son of Dardanus, son of Jupiter, of the race of Ham, the accursed son who saw his father Noah and mocked him. Tros had two sons, Ilius and Asaracus. Ilius first founded the city of Ilium, that is Troy, and then begot Lamedon, who was the father of Priam. But Asaracus begot Capen, who was the father of Anchises. Anchises begot Aeneas, who was the father of Ascanius. †
†So I found it, as I have written it on this page, for you, Samuel, the child of my master, the priest Beulan. But this genealogy is not written in any book of Britain, but was in the writing of the writer's mind. †

11. Aeneas reigned three years among the Latins. Ascanius reigned 37 years, and after him Silvius, son of Aeneas, reigned 12 years, . Postumus 39 years; and from him the kings of the Albani are called Silvii; and Britto was his brother.

When Britto reigned in Britain, Eli the High Priest ruled in Israel, and then the Ark of the Covenant was taken by foreigners. Postumus, his brother, ruled among the Latins.

12. After an interval of many years, not less than 800, Picts came and occupied the islands called Orkney, and later from the islands they wasted many lands, and occupied those in the northern part of Britain, and they still live there to-day. They held and hold a third part of Britain to this day.

13. But later the Irish came from Spain to Ireland more recently. Partholon came first with a thousand, men and women, and they grew until they were four thousand, and a plague came upon them, and in one week they all died, and there remained not a one of them. Nemet, son of Agnoman, came second to Ireland, and is said to have sailed over the sea for a year and a half, and then made port in Ireland, by shipwreck, and stayed there many years, and set sail again with his people, and returned to Spain. Later, three sons of a warrior of Spain came with thirty keels between them, and thirty wives in each keel, and stayed there for the space of a year. Later, they saw a glass tower in the midst of the sea, and saw men upon the tower, and sought to speak with them, but they never replied; and in the one year they made haste to attack the tower, with all their keels and all their women, except one keel, that was shipwrecked, in which were thirty men and as many women. The other ships sailed to attack the tower, and when they all disembarked on the shore that was around the tower, the sea overwhelmed them, and they were drowned, and not one of them escaped; and from the crew of that one ship that was left behind because of the shipwreck all Ireland was filled, to the present day; and afterwards they came over gradually from Spain, and held many districts.

† There is however nothing certain about the history of the origins of the Irish. †

14. Later came the Kindred of Eight and lived there with all their race in Britain until today. Istoreth son of Istorinus held Dal Riada with his people. Bolg with his people held the Isle of Man, and other islands about. The sons of Liathan prevailed in the country of the Demetians, †where the city of Mynyw is†, and in other countries, that is Gower

[and] Kidwelly, until they were expelled by Cunedda, and by his sons, from all countries in Britain.

15. If anyone wants to know when Ireland was inhabited and when it was deserted, this is what the Irish scholars have told me. When the children of Israel crossed through the Red Sea, the Egyptians came and pursued them and were drowned, as may be read in the Law. Among the Egyptians was a nobleman of Scythia, with a great following, who had been expelled from his kingdom, and was there when the Egyptians were drowned, but did not join in the pursuit of the children of God. The survivors took counsel to expel him, lest he should attack their kingdom and occupy it, for their strength had been drowned in the Red Sea; †for his wife was Scotta, the daughter of Pharoah, from whom Scotia, Ireland, is said to be named.† He was expelled and he wandered for 42 years through Africa, and they came to the Altars of the Philistines, by the Salt Lake, and through Rusicade and the Mountains of Axaria, and by the river Muluya, and crossed through Morocco to the Pillars of Hercules, and sailed over the Tyrrhene Sea, and came to Spain, and there they lived for many years, and grew and multiplied exceedingly, and their people multiplied exceedingly. After they had come to Spain, and 1002 years after the Egyptians had been drowned in the Red Sea, they came to the country of Dal Riada, at the time when Brutus was ruling among the Romans, with whom the Consuls began, and then the Tribunes of the Plebs and the Dictators. The Consuls however held the State for 447 years, which had previously suffered the rule of Kings.

The British came to Britain in the Third Age of the world; but the Irish secured Ireland in the Fourth Age. But the Irish, who are in the west, and Picts from the north, fought together in a united assault on the British unremittingly, for the British were unused to weapons; and after a long interval the Romans secured the monarchy of the whole world.

16. From the year when the Saxons first came to Britain to the fourth year of king Mervyn, 429 years are reckoned; from the birth of the Lord until the coming of Patrick to the Irish are 405 years. From the death of Patrick to the death of Saint Brigit are 60 years; from the birth of Columba to the death of Brigit are 4 years.

Starting point of the calculation. 23 cycles of 19 years from the Incarnation of the Lord until the coming of Patrick to Ireland; these years number 438. From the coming of Patrick to the present 19 year cycle there are 22 cycles, that is 421 years, two years in the Ogdoad until this present year.

21

17.   I found another explanation about Brutus in the old books of
our elders. The three sons of Noah divided the world into three parts after
the Flood. Sem extended his boundaries in Asia, Ham in Africa, Japheth
in Europe.

The first man who came to Europe was Alanus, of the race of
Japheth, with his three sons, whose names are Hessitio, Armenon, and
Negue. Hessitio had four sons, Francus, Romanus, Britto and Albanus;
Armenon had five sons, Gothus, Walagothus, Gepidus, Burgundus,
Langobardus; Negue had three sons, Vandalus, Saxo, Bavarus. From
Hessitio derive four peoples, the Franks, the Latins, the Albans and
the British; from Armenon five, the Goths, the Walagoths, the Gepids,
the Burgundians, the Langobards; from Negue four, the Bavarians, the
Vandals, the Saxons and the Thuringians. These peoples are subdivided
throughout Europe. Alanus is said to have been son of Fetebir, son of
Ougomun, son of Thous, son of Boib, son of Simeon, son of Mair, son
of †Ethach, son of† Aurthach, son of †Ecthet, son of† Oth, son of
Abir, son of Rhea, son of Ezra, son of Izrau, son of Baath, son of
Iobaath, son of Javan, son of Japheth, son of Noah, son of Lamech, son
of Methuselah, son of Enoch, son of Jared, son of Mahalaleel, son of
Cainan, son of Enos, son of Seth, son of Adam, son of the Living God.
This learning I found in the tradition of our elders.

18.   The first inhabitants of Britain were the British, from Brutus.
Brutus was the son of Hessitio, Hessitio of Alanus. Alanus was the son
of Rhea Silvia, daughter of Numa Pompilius, son of Ascanius. Ascanius
was the son of Aeneas, son of Anchises, son of Trous, son of Dardanus,
son of Elishah, son of Javan, son of Japheth. Japheth had seven sons; first
Gomer, †from whom the Gauls; second Magog , from whom the Scythians
and the Goths; third Madai†, from whom the Medes; fourth Javan, from
whom the Greeks; fifth Tubal, from whom †the Iberians†, the Spaniards
and the Italians; sixth Meshach, from whom the Cappadocians; seventh
Tiras, from whom the Thracians. These are the sons of Japheth, son of
Noah, son of Lamech.

[ROMAN BRITAIN]

19.   Now I return to the point where I digressed. When the Romans
acquired the mastery of the whole world they sent legates to the British,
to demand hostages and taxes from them, such as they received from
all countries and islands. But the British were arrogant and turbulent,
and spurned the Roman legates. Then Julius Caesar, who had been the
first to receive and hold sole power, was extremely angry, and came to
Britain with sixty keels, and made land in the Thames estuary, where

22

his ships suffered shipwreck, while he was fighting with Dolabella, who was proconsul to the British king whose name was Belinus, son of Minocan, who occupied all the islands of the Tyrrhene Sea, and Julius returned without victory, his soldiers killed and his ships wrecked.

20.   He came again, after an interval of three years, with a great army and three hundred keels, and reached the estuary of the river called Thames. There they fought a battle, and many of his horses and his soldiers fell, because the aforementioned proconsul put iron stakes and 'battle seed', that is, caltrops, in the river ford. This unseen contrivance was a decisive danger to the Roman soldiers, and they went away without peace on that occasion. The third battle was fought near the place called Trinovantum, and Julius won empire over the British nation 47 years before the birth of Christ, 5,215 years from the beginning of the world.

Julius therefore was the first to come to Britain, and hold the kingdom and the nation, and the Romans decreed that in his honour the month Quintilis should be called July. But on the Ides of March Gaius Julius Caesar was killed in the senate house; and when Octavian Augustus held the monarchy of the whole world, he alone received taxation from Britain; as Vergil says *The embroidered British lift the purple stage-curtains.*

21.   After him the second emperor to come was Claudius, and he ruled in Britain 48 years after the coming of Christ, and fought a great and bloody battle, not without loss to his troops, but however he was victorious in Britain. Afterwards, he went with his keels to the Orkney Islands and conquered them and made them tributary. In his time, the payment of taxation by Britain to the Romans ceased, but taxes were paid to British emperors. He reigned 13 years and 8 months, and his monument is to be seen at Mogantia in Lombardy; while he was on his way to Rome, he died there.

22.   Lucius, the British king, received baptism, with all the underkings of the British nation, 167 years after the coming of Christ, after a legation had been sent by the Roman emperors and by Eucharistus, the Roman Pope.

23.   Severus was the third to cross to the British. To protect the subject provinces from barbarian invasion, he built a wall rampart there, which is called Guaul in the British language, from sea to sea across the width of Britain, that is for 132 miles †from Penguaul, a place which is called

23

Cenail in Irish, Peneltun in English, to the estuary of the Clyde and Caer Pentaloch, where it finishes. The said Severus built it ruggedly, but in vain. The emperor Carausius rebuilt it later, and fortified it with 7 forts, between the two estuaries, and a Round House of polished stone, on the banks of the river Carron, which takes its name from him; he erected a triumphal arch to commemorate his victory†. Severus ordered the wall to be built between the British and the Picts and Irish, because the Irish from the west and the Picts from the north were fighting against the British, for they were at peace with each other. Not long afterwards, Severus died in Britain; †he was killed at York with his generals†.

24.   The fourth emperor was Carausius, who was a tyrant, and came to Britain tyrannically. He became tyrant because of the killing of Severus, and along with all the generals of the Roman nation who were with him in Britain, he struck down all the little kings of the British, and took the purple over Britain.

25.   The fifth [to come to Britain] was Constantine, son of Constantine the Great, and there he died. His tomb is to be seen by the city called Caer Seint, as the letters on its stonework show. He sowed three seeds, of gold, of silver, and of bronze, on the pavement of that city, that no man should ever live there poor; its other name is Minmanton.

26.   The sixth emperor to reign in Britain was Maximus. From his time, the consuls began, and they were never again called Caesars. In his time too the powers and miracles of Saint Martin flowered, and Martin spoke with Maximus.

27.   The seventh emperor to reign in Britain was Maxim(ian)us. He went forth from Britain with all the troops of the British and killed Gratian, the king of the Romans, and held the empire of all Europe. He refused to send the soldiers who had gone forth with him back to Britain, to their wives and children and lands, but gave them many districts from the lake on top of Mount Jove to the city called Quentovic, as far as the Western Mass, that is the Western Ridge. †For the Armorican British, who are overseas, went forth there with the tyrant Maximus on his campaign, and, since they were unwilling to return, they destroyed the western parts of Gaul to the ground, and did not leave alive those who piss against the wall. They married their wives and daughters and cut out their tongues, lest their descendants should learn their mothers' tongue. That is why we call them in our language 'Letewicion', that is, half-dumb, because their speech is muddled†. They are the Armorican British, and they

never came back, even to the present day. That is why Britain has been occupied by foreigners, and the citizens driven out, until God shall give them help.

In the ancient tradition of our elders, there were seven emperors in Britain, but the Romans say there were nine. The eighth was another Severus, who spent some time in Britain, and went to Rome for a while, and there died. The ninth was Constantius. He reigned 16 years in Britain, and in the sixteenth year of his reign he died in Britain [*he was the last emperor to rule the British in Britain*].

28.   Hitherto the Romans had ruled the British for 409 years. But the British overthrew the rule of the Romans, and paid them no taxes, and did not accept their kings to reign over them, and the Romans did not dare to come to Britain to rule anymore, for the British had killed their generals.

29.   A second report of the tyrant Maximianus must be reported. Gratian ruled 6 years with his brother Valentinian, and bishop Ambrose of Milan was famous in catholic teaching. Valentinian reigned 8 years with Theodosius. The Synod of Constantinople, in which all the heresies were condemned, was held by 318 Fathers. Then the priest Jerome of Bethlehem was famous throughout the world. While Gratian ruled throughout the world, Maximus was made emperor in Britain by a mutiny. He soon crossed to Gaul, and overcame Gratian, who was betrayed at Paris by his commander-in-chief, Merobaudes, and fled, and was taken at Lyon and killed. Maximus made his son Victor his colleague. Bishop Martin of Tours was famous for his great powers. After a long lapse of time, he [Maximus] was stopped by the consuls Valentinian and Theodosius at the third milestone from Aquileia, deprived of his royal raiment, and sentenced to execution. His son Victor was killed in Gaul in the same year by Count Arbogast.

30.   The Roman generals were killed by the British on three occasions. But when the British were harassed by the barbarian nations, that is the Irish and the Picts, they implored the Romans to help. When their envoys were seen in deep distress, they made their appearance with dust on their heads, carrying with them great gifts for the Roman consuls, as an admission of the crime of killing the Roman generals. The consuls received their thankofferings, and they promised to swear to accept the yoke of Roman law, although it was harsh.

25

The Romans came with a great army to help them, and placed emperors in Britain; and when the emperor was established with his generals, the armies went back to Rome, and came and went in alternation over 348 years. But the British killed the Roman generals, because of the weight of the empire, and later asked their help. The Romans came to bring help to the empire and defend it, and deprived Britain of her gold and silver and bronze, and all her precious raiment and honey, and went back in great triumph.

[THE FIFTH CENTURY]

[THE KENTISH CHRONICLE, PART 1]

31.   It came to pass that after this war between the British and the Romans, when their generals were killed, and after the killing of the tyrant Maximus and the end of the Roman Empire in Britain, the British went in fear for 40 years. Vortigern ruled in Britain, and during his rule in Britain he was under pressure, from fear of the Picts and the Irish, and of a Roman invasion, and, not least, from dread of Ambrosius.Then came three keels, driven into exile from Germany. In them were the brothers Horsa and Hengest, sons of Wichtgils, son of Witta, son of Wechta, son of Woden, son of Frealaf, son of Fredulf, son of Finn, *son of* Folcwald, son of Geta, who said they were son of God; but He was not the God of Gods, Amen, the God of Hosts, but one of the idols they worshipped. Vortigern welcomed them, and handed over to them the island that in their language is called Thanet, in British Ruoihm.

When Gratian ruled for the second time with Equitius, the Saxons were received by Vortigern, 347 years after the Passion of Christ.

[THE LIFE OF SAINT GERMANUS, PART 1]

32.   In his time Germanus came to preach in Britain, and became famous among them by his many powers, and many were saved through him, and many came to perdition.

I have decided that some of the miracles that God wrought through him should be recorded.

The first of his miracles.

There was a wicked king called Benlli, a great tyrant. The holy man wanted to visit him, and to hasten to preach to the wicked king. But when the man of God came to the city gate with his companions, the porter came to greet them, and they sent him to the king; and the

26

king answered roughly with an oath, saying 'Even if they are here, and stay here till the end of the year, they shall never enter within my city.' While they were waiting for the gate-keeper to bring them the tyrant's message, the day turned to evening, and night drew near, and they knew not where to go. Then one of the king's servants came from within the city, and bowed before the man of God, and told him all the tyrant's words; and invited them to go out with them to his own house. They went out with him, and he welcomed them. But he had no animal of any kind, except a cow with a calf, and he killed the calf, and cooked it, and placed it before them. But saint Germanus gave order that none of its bones should be broken; and so it was done, and on the morrow the calf was found well, alive and unharmed with its mother.

33.   They rose in the morning, and sought again to greet the tyrant. But while they prayed and waited outside the gate of the fortress, behold, a man came running, the sweat dripping from the top of his head to the soles of his feet. He bowed before them, and saint Germanus said 'Dost thou believe in the Holy Trinity?', and he answered 'I believe,' and was baptised.He kissed him, and said 'Go in peace. Within this hour shalt thou die, and the Angels of God await thee in the skies, and thou shalt proceed with them to God, in Whom thou believest.' He entered joyfully within the fortress, and the prefect held him, and bound him, and he was led before the tyrant and slain, for it was the custom of the abominable tyrant that anyone who had not arrived within the fortress for his service before sunrise should be slain. They stayed the whole day by the gate of the city, but did not succeed in greeting the tyrant.

34.   The aforesaid servant was there, as was usual, and saint Germanus said to him 'Take care that not a single one of your men stays this night in the fortress.' So he went back into the fortress and brought out his sons, who were nine in number, and they came back with him to the aforesaid lodging. Saint Germanus told them to stay fasting within closed doors, saying 'Be watchful, and if anything happens in the fortress, do not look, but continue praying and calling upon your God without pause.' After a short interval, night fire fell from heaven, and burnt the fortress and all the men who were with the tyrant, and they have never been seen to this day, and the fortress has not been rebuilt, even to this day.

35   On the morrow, the man who had been their host believed and was baptised with all his sons, and the whole country with him. His name was Cadell. Germanus blessed him, and in addition said 'From

your seed a king shall not fail †for ever† (for he is Cadell Ddyrnllug), and you
alone shall be king from this day.' So it was, and so was fulfilled the saying
of the prophet 'He raiseth up the poor out of the dust, and lifteth up the
beggar from the dunghill, to set them among princes, and to make them
inherit the throne of glory.' According to saint Germanus' words, he was
made a king from a servant, and all his sons were make kings, and from
their seed the whole country of Powys is ruled, even to this day.

[THE KENTISH CHRONICLE, PART 2]

36.   And it came to pass, after the English were encamped in the aforesaid island of Thanet, the aforesaid king promised to supply them with
food and clothing without fail; and they agreed, and promised to fight
bravely against his enemies. But the barbarians multiplied their numbers,
and the British could not feed them. When they demanded the promised
food and clothing, the British said 'We cannot give you food and clothing,
for your numbers are grown. Go away, for we do not need your help.'
So they took counsel with their elders, to break the peace.

37.   But Hengest was an experienced man, shrewd and skilful. Sizing up
the king's impotence, and the military weakness of his people, he held a
council, and said to the British king 'We are few; if you wish, we can send
home and invite warriors from the fighting men of our country, that the
number who fight for you and your people may be larger.' The king
ordered it to be done, and envoys were sent across the sea, and came back
with sixteen keels, with picked warriors in them. In one of the keels came
Hengest's daughter, a beautiful and very handsome girl. When the
keels had arrived, Hengest held a banquet for Vortigern, and his   men and
his interpreter, whose name was Ceretic, and he told the girl to serve their
wine and spirits. They all got exceedingly drunk. When they were drinking,
Satan entered into Vortigern's heart, and made him love the girl. Through
his interpreter he asked her father for her hand, saying 'Ask of me what
you will, even to the half of my kingdom.'

Hengest took counsel with the elders of Angeln, to decide what they
should ask of the king for the girl, and they all agreed to ask for the country
that in their language is called Canturguoralen, in ours Kent. So he granted
it to them, although Gwyrangon was ruling in Kent, and did not know that
his kingdom was being handed over to the heathens, and that he was himself
given secretly into their power on his own. So the girl was given in marriage
to Vortigern, and he slept with her, and loved her deeply.

28

38.   Hengest said to Vortigern 'I am your father, and will be your
adviser. Never ignore my advice, and you will never fear conquest by any
man or any people, for my people are strong. I will invite my son and his
cousin to fight against the Irish, for they are fine warriors. Give them lands
in the north about the Wall that is called Guaul.' So he told him to invite
them, and he invited Octha and Ebissa, with forty keels. They sailed round
the Picts and wasted the Orkney Islands, and came and occupied many
districts beyond the Frenessican Sea, as far as the borders of the Picts.
So Hengest gradually brought over more and more keels, until they left the
islands †whence† they came uninhabited; and as his people grew in strength
and numbers, they came to the aforesaid city of the Kentishmen.

[THE LIFE OF SAINT GERMANUS, PART 2]

39.   Then, on top of all his misdeeds, Vortigern took his daughter to wife,
and begot a daughter upon her. When this was made known to saint
Germanus, he came with all the clergy of Britain to accuse him. When the
great Synod of the clergy and laity met together in a single council, the
king told his daughter beforehand to come to the meeting, and put her son
in the lap of Germanus, and say that he was the child's father. The woman
did as she was told, but Germanus took the child kindly, and addressed him
'I will be your father, and will not send you away, unless a razor and
scissors and comb are given me, and you are permitted to give them to
your father after the flesh.' The boy heard him, and turned to his grand-
father Vortigern, his father after the flesh, and said to him 'You are my
father. Crop my head, and the hair of my head.' But he was silent, and
said nothing, and refused to answer the boy. He got up in great anger, and
fled from the face of saint Germanus, and was accursed, and was condemned
by saint Germanus and the whole council of the British.

[THE TALE OF EMRYS]

40.   Then the king invited his wizards to him, and asked them what was
to be done. They said 'Go to the farthest borders of your kingdom, and
find a fortified stronghold to defend yourself, for the people whom you
received into your kingdom has turned against you, and will seek to slay
you treacherously, and will occupy all the countries you loved, and all
your people, after your death. Then the king came with his wizards to
seek the stronghold, and encompassed many countries and many
provinces, and did not find it, and at last they came to the country called
Gwynedd; and when he was exploring in the mountains of Eryri, †that is,
in English, Snowdon,† he at length reached a place in one of the
mountains that was suitable for building a stronghold. So his wizards
said to him 'Make a stronghold in this place, for it will be for ever safest

against the barbarian peoples.' So he assembled his workmen, that it the
masons, and assembled the timber and stones, and when he had assembled
all the material, it disappeared in a single night. Three times he ordered
it to be assembled, and it was nowhere to be seen. So he summoned his
wizards, and interrogated them about the cause of the evil, and how it had
come about. They answered 'Unless you find a child without a father, and
he is killed, and the stronghold is sprinkled with his blood, it will never be
built at all.'

41.   So he sent envoys from the council of the wizards through the
whole of Britain, to discover whether there was a child without a father.
As they explored all the provinces and many countries, they came to
Maes Elledi, in the country called Glywysing. Boys were playing ball [there].
Two of them were quarrelling and one said to the other 'You have no
father, you will come to no good.' So they questioned the boys closely
about him, and asked his mother if he had a father. She denied it, saying
'I do not know how he was conceived in my womb, but one thing I do
know is that I have never known a man', and she swore to them that he
had no father. So they took him with them and introduced him to
king Vortigern.

42.   So on the morrow a meeting was held, for the killing of the boy.
But the boy said to the king† 'Why did your men bring me to you?' The
king replied 'So that you could be killed, and your blood sprinkled around
this fortress, so that it can be built.' The boy replied† 'Who told you that?'
'My wizards told me' said the king. 'Call them to me' said the boy. So the
wizards were summoned, and the boy said 'Who revealed to you that this
fortress is to be sprinkled with my blood, and that if it is not sprinkled with
my blood, it will never be built at all? Who proclaimed this about me, for
you to know it? And the boy went on 'Now I will explain it to you, oh king,
and fully satisfy you of the truth. But I must question your wizards. What
is in the foundation of this place? I want them to show you what there is
under the foundations.' But they said 'We do not know.' He said 'I know.
There is a lake in the midst of the foundation; come and dig, and you will
find it.' They came and dug, and it fell in. The boy said to the wizards
'Reveal to me what there is in the lake.' But they were silent, and could not
tell him. So he said to them 'I will show you. You will find that there are
two vessels there.' They came and saw that it was so, and the boy said to
the wizards 'What is shut up in the vessels?' But they were silent and could
not tell him. But he declared 'There is a cloth in the midst of them;
separate them and you will find it.' The king ordered them to be separated
and a folded cloth was found, as he had said. He asked the wizards again
'Tell me what is inside the cloth.' But they knew not. So he showed them

'Two worms are in it, one white the other red. Unfold the cloth.' They unfolded it, and found two worms, asleep. The boy said 'Wait and see what the worms do.' The worms began to drive each other out. One used his shoulders to drive the other on to a half of the cloth. This they did three times; then the red worm was seen to be weaker, and then was stronger than the white, and drove him beyond the edge of the cloth. The one pursued the other across the lake, and the cloth vanished.

Then the boy asked the wizards 'What is the meaning of this remarkable sign, that happened on the cloth?' They admitted 'We do not know.' The boy answered 'This mystery is revealed to me, and I will make it plain to you. The cloth represents your kingdom, and the two worms are two dragons. The red worm is your dragon, and the lake represents the world. But the white one is the dragon of the people who have seized many peoples and countries in Britain, and will reach almost from sea to sea; but later our people will arise, and will valiantly throw the English people across the sea. But do you go forth from this fortress, for you cannot build it, and travel over many provinces, to find a safe fortress, and I will stay here.' Then the king asked the lad 'What is your name?' He replied 'I am called Ambrosius', that is, he was shown to be Emrys the Overlord. The king asked 'What family do you come from?' and the answered† 'My father is one of the consuls of the Roman people.' So the king gave him the fortress, with all the kingdoms of the western part of Britain, and he went himself with his wizards to the northern part, and came to the region called 'Gwynessi', and there he built a city, that is called by his name, Caer Gwrtheyrn.

[THE KENTISH CHRONICLE, PART 3]

43. Meanwhile, Vortigern's son Vortimer fought vigorously against Hengest and Horsa and their people, and expelled them as far as the aforesaid island called Thanet, and there three times shut them up and besieged them, attacking, threatening and terrifying them. So they sent envoys overseas to Germany to summon keels with a vast number of fighting men. And afterwards they used to fight against the kings of one nation, sometimes victoriously advancing their frontiers, sometimes being defeated and expelled.

44. Vortimer fought four keen battles against them. The first battle was on the river Darenth. The second battle was at the ford called Episford in their language, Rhyd yr afael in ours, and there fell Horsa and also Vortigern's son Cateyrn. The third battle was fought in the open country by the Inscribed Stone on the shore of the Gallic Sea. The barbarians were beaten and he was victorious. They fled to their keels and were drowned as they clambered aboard them like women.

31

But Vortimer soon after died. Before he died he told his followers to set his tomb by the coast, in the port from which (the English) had departed, saying 'I entrust it to you. Wherever else they may hold a British port or may have settled, they will never again live in this land.' But they ignored his command and did not bury him where he had told them: †for he is buried in Lincoln. But if they had kept his command, there is no doubt that they would have obtained whatever they wished through the prayers of saint Germanus.†

45. But the barbarians returned in force, for Vortigern was their friend, because of his wife, and none was resolute to drive them out; for they occupied Britain not because of their strength, but because it was the will of God. Who can resist the will of God, even if he tries. The lord did what He would, for He rules and governs all the nations.

So it came to pass that after the death of Vortimer, son of king Vortigern, and after the return of Hengest and his hosts, they instigated a treacherous plan, to trick Vortigern and his army. They sent envoys to ask for peace and make a permanent treaty. Vortigern called a council of his elders to examine what they should do. Ultimately one opinion prevailed with all, that they should make peace. The envoys went back, and conference was convened, wher the two sides, British and English, should meet, unarmed, to confirm the treaty.

46. But Hengest told all his followers to hide their daggers under their feet in their shoes, saying 'When I call out to you and say *"English, draw your knives"*, take your daggers from your shoes and fall upon them, and stand firm against them. But do not kill the king; keep him alive, for my daughter's sake, whom I wedded to him, for it is better for us that he be ransomed from us.' So the conference assembled, and the English, friendly in their words, but wolfish in heart and deed, sat down, like allies, man beside man. Hengest cried out as he had said, and all the three hundred Seniors of king Vortigern were murdered, and the king alone was taken and held prisoner. To save his life, he ceded several districts, namely Essex and Sussex, †together with Middlesex and other districts that they chose and designated.†

[THE LIFE OF SAINT GERMANUS, PART 3]

47. But saint Germanus preached at Vortigern, to convert him to his lord, and to separate him from his illicit union. But he fled in desperation to the country that is called Gwerthrynion after him, and hid there with his wives. So saint Germanus followed him with all the British clergy, and stayed there forty days and forty nights, standing upon a rock day and night and beseeching him. Then Vortigern withdrew in disgrace to the fortress of Vortigern, which is in the country of the Demetians, on the river Teifi. Saint Germanus

followed him, as before, and stayed there fasting with all the clergy for three days and as many nights to achieve his end, and on the fourth night, about midnight, the whole fortress was suddenly destroyed by fire sent from heaven, and the fire of heaven burned. Vortigern was destroyed with all who were with him, and with all his wives. This is the end of Vortigern, as I found it in the book of the Blessed Germanus; but others have different versions.

48. When he was hated for his sin, †because he received the English people†, by all men of his own nation, mighty and humble, slave and free, monk and layman, poor and great, he wandered from place to place until at last his heart broke, and he died without honour. Others say that the earth opened and swallowed him up on the night when his fortress was burnt about him, for no trace was ever found of those who were burned with him in the fortress.

He had three sons, whose names are Vortimer, who fought against the barbarians, as I have described above, the second, Cateyrn; the third, Pascent, who ruled in the two countries called Builth and Gwerthrynion after his father's death, by permission of Ambrosius, who was the †great† king among all the kings of the British nation. A fourth son was Faustus, who was born to him by his daughter. Saint Germanus baptised him, and brought him up, and taught him, and he founded a great monastery on the banks of a river, called Riez, that stands to this day. He also had one daughter, who was the mother of saint Faustus.

49. This is his genealogy, traced backwards to the beginning. Ffernfeal, who now rules in the countries of Builth and Gwerthrynion, is son of Tewdwr. Theodore is king of the country of Builth, the son of Pascent, son of Gwyddgant, son of Moriud, son of Eldat, son of Elaeth, son of Paul, son of Meuric [son of Idnerth], son of Briacat, son of Pascent, son of Vortigern the Thin, son of Vitalis, son of Vitalinus, son of Gloiu. Bonus, Paul, Mauron and Vitalinus were four brothers, sons of Gloiu, who built the great city on the banks of the river Severn that is called in the British Caer Gloiu, in English Gloucester. Enough has been said of Vortigern and his family.

50. After his death, saint Germanus returned to his own country.

[THE LIFE OF SAINT PATRICK]

At that time, saint Patrick was a captive among the Irish, and his master was named Milchu, and he was his swineherd, and [he was] in the seventeenth year of his age. He returned from captivity, and by God's will was later schooled in divine letters, and came to Rome and stayed there for a long time. He went through a course of reading and of studying the mysteries of God and of the books of the holy scriptures. When he had been there seven years, Palladius was sent by Celestine, Bishop and Pope of Rome, as the first bishop to convert the Irish to Christ. But God hindered him with various misfortunes, for no one can acquire anything on earth, unless it be given to him from heaven above. So Palladius left Ireland and came to Britain and died there, in the land of the Picts.

51.   When the death of bishop Palladius was known, Patrick was sent as second legate, in the reign of Theodosius and Valentinian, by Celestine the Roman Pope and by an angel of God named Victor, on the urgent advice of the holy bishop Germanus, to convert the Irish to the faith of Christ. Germanus sent with him an elder, Segitius, to a wonderful man, the chief bishop Amator, who lived nearby. There the holy bishop, knowing all that would happen to him in the future, received the rank of bishop from Amator, and took the name Patrick, for he had formerly been called Maun. Auxilius, Iserninus and others were ordained with him, in a lower rank.

52.   Then, when they had received blessing, and completed all else in the name of the Holy Trinity, they embarked on a waiting ship, and sailed to Britain, and preached there for not many days; avoiding all digressions on their journey, they sailed down the Irish Sea with all speed and a favourable wind with their ship. The ship was laden with overseas marvels and spiritual treasures, and they reached Ireland, and he baptised them.

53.   From the beginning of the world to the baptism of the Irish there are 5,330 years. In the fifth year of king Loegaire he began to preach the faith of Christ.

54.   So saint Patrick preached the Gospel of Christ to foreign nations for forty years, working wonders like the Apostles, bringing light to the blind, cleansing lepers, making the deaf hear, chasing demons from the bodies wherein they dwelt, raising the dead, to the number of nine, ransoming many captives of both sexes by gifts of his own. He wrote three hundred and sixty five or more alphabets, and also founded the same number of churches, three hundred and sixty five. He consecrated three hundred and sixty five or more bishops, and the spirit of God was in them; and ordained as many as three thousand priests, and converted and baptised twelve thousand men to the faith of Christ in a single region, Connacht, and baptised on one day seven kings, who were sons of Amolgaid. He fasted for forty days and forty nights on the summit of Eile hill, that is Cruachan Eile; and on that hill that reached to the skies, he gently asked three petitions for those of the Irish who had received the faith. The Irish say that the first of his petitions is that every-

one should enter into repentance, even in extreme old age; and second that they should not be destroyed by barbarians for ever; the third, that none of the Irish should survive to the Advent of Judgment, but that in honour of Patrick they should be brought to their end seven years before the judgment. On that hill he blessed the peoples of Ireland, and he climbed it in order to pray for them and to see the fruit of his labour. And there came to him innumerable birds of many colours for him to bless, which signifies that all the saints of the Irish of both sexes should come to him on the Day of Judgment, to their father and teacher, to follow him to Judgment. Afterwards, he passed over in good old age, wherefore he now has joy for ever and ever. Amen.

55.   In four ways Patrick is like Moses; in talking with an angel in the burning bush; secondly, he fasted on a mountain for forty days and forty nights; thirdly, both alike were 120 years old; fourthly, no man knows his tomb, for he was buried in secret, no one knowing where. He was 15 years in captivity, and in his twenty fifth year he was appointed by the holy bishop Amator, and he preached in Ireland for 85 years. The matter demands that more should be said of Saint Patrick, but nevertheless I must be brief, to shorten my tale.

[THE CAMPAIGNS OF ARTHUR]

56.   At that time the English increased their numbers and grew in Britain. On Hengest's death, his son Octha came down from the north of Britain to the kingdom of the Kentishmen, and from him are sprung the kings of the Kentishmen. Then Arthur fought against them in those days, together with the kings of the British; but he was their leader in battle.

The first battle was at the mouth of the river called Glein. The second, the third, the fourth and the fifth were on another river, called the Douglas, which is in the country of Lindsey. The sixth battle was on the river called Bassas. The seventh battle was in Celyddon Forest, that is, the Battle of Celyddon Coed. The eighth battle was in Guinnion fort, and in it Arthur carried the image of the holy Mary, the everlasting Virgin, on his [shield,] and the heathen were put to flight on that day, and there was a great slaughter upon them, through the power of Our Lord Jesus Christ and the power of the holy Virgin Mary, his mother. The ninth battle was fought in the city of the Legion. The tenth battle was fought on the bank of the river called Tryfrwyd. The eleventh battle was on the hill called Agned. The twelfth battle was on Badon Hill and in it nine hundred and sixty men fell in one day, from a single charge of Arthur's, and no one laid them low save he alone; and he was victorious in all his campaigns.

When they were defeated in all their campaigns, the English sought help from Germany, and continually and considerably increased their numbers, and they brought over their kings from Germany to rule over them in Britain, until the time when Ida reigned, who was the son of Eobba. He was the first king in Bernicia, that is, in Berneich.

[THE SIXTH AND SEVENTH CENTURIES]
[THE NORTHERN HISTORY, PART 1]

57.   [THE KINGS OF THE BERNICIANS 1] Woden begot Baeldeg, begot Beornec, begot Gechbrond, begot Alusa, begot Ingui, begot Aethelbert, begot Eobba, begot Ida. Ida had twelve sons, named Adda, Aethelric, Theodoric, Edric, Theodohare, Osmera, and one queen, Bearnoch, [who was their mother; and six sons from his concubines, Occa,] Ealric, [Ecca, Oswald, Sogor, Sogethere.] Aethelric begot Alfred; he is Aethelferth the Artful, and he had seven sons, named Eanfrid, Oswald, Oswy, Osguid, Osgudu, Oslaph, Offa. Oswy begot Aldfrith and Aelfwin and Egferth. That is the Egferth who fought a battle against his cousin, the king of the Picts, named Bridei, and there he fell with all the strength of his army, and the Picts and their king were victorious, and the English thugs never grew [strong enough] from the time of that battle to exact tribute from the Picts. It was called the battle of Llyn Garan. But Oswy had two wives, one of whom was called Rieinmellt, daughter of Royth, son of Rhun, and the other was called Eanfeld, daughter of Edwin, son of Aelle.

[SOUTHERN ENGLISH GENEALOGIES]

58.   [THE GENEALOGY OF THE KINGS OF KENT] Hengest begot Octha, begot Ossa, begot Eormenric, begot Aethelbert, begot Eadbald, begot Erconbert, begot Egbert.

The Origin of the kings of the East Angles.
59. Woden begot Casser, begot Tytmon, begot Trygils, begot Rothmund, begot Hryp, begot Wilhelm Guechan. He was the first to rule over the people of the East Angles. Guechan begot Wuffa, begot Tytill, begot Eni begot [Aethelhere], begot Aldwulf, begot Aethelric.

60.   [THE GENEALOGY OF THE MERCIANS] Woden begot Watholgeot, begot Waga, begot Wihtlaeg, begot Waermund, begot Offa, begot Angen[geot], begot Eomer, [begot Icel, begot cnebba, begot Cynewald, begot Creoda], begot Pybba. Pybba had twelve sons, two of whom are better known to

me than the others, namely Penda and Eobba. Aethelred was the son of Penda; Penda was the son of Pybba. Aethelbald was son of Alweo, son of Eobba, [brother] of Penda, son of Pybba. Egferth son of Offa, son of Thingfrith, son of Eanwulf, son of Osmond, son of Eobba, son of Pybba.

61.   THE KINGS OF THE DEIRANS. Woden begot Baeldeg, [begot] Brand, begot Sigegar, [begot Swebdaeg, begot Sigegeat,] begot Saebald, begot Saefugl, begot Soemil. He first seperated Deira from Bernicia. Soemil begot Swaerta, [begot Westerfalca,] begot Wilgsil, begot Wyscfrea, begot Yffe, begot Aelle, [begot] Edwin. Osfrid and Eadfrid were the two sons of Edwin, and they fell with him at the battle of Meicen, and the kingdom was never revived from their stock, for none of their line survived that battle, but they were all killed with him by the army of Catwallaun, king of the country of Gwynedd.

[THE KINGS OF THE BERNICIANS, 2] Oswy begot Egferth; he is Egferth, [the brother of] Aelfwin, [who] begot Oslac, begot Aldhun, begot Aethelsige (?), begot Ecca (?), begot Oslaph. Ida begot Aethelric, begot Ecgulf, begot Leodwald, begot Eata, (he is Eata Glin Mawr), begot Edbert and Egbert the Bishop, who was the first of their nation.
    Ida son of Eobba, held the countries in the north of Britain, that is, north of the Humber Sea, and reigned twelve years, and joined Din Guaire to Bernicia, †and these two countries became one country, namely Deur and Berneich, in English, Deira and Bernicia.†

62.   At that time Outigern then fought bravely against the English nation. Then Talhaearn Tad Awen was famed in poetry; and Aneirin and Taliesin and Bluchbard and Cian, known as Gueinth Guaut, were all simultaneously famed in British verse.

    King Maelgwn the Great was reigning among the British, in Gwynedd, for his ancestors, Cunedda, with his sons, to the number of eight, had come from the north, from the country called Manaw Gododdin, 146 years before Maelgwn reigned, and expelled the Irish from these countries, with immense slaughter, so that they never again returned to inhabit them.

63.   Adda, son of Ida, reigned 8 years; Aethelric, son of Ida, reigned 4 years. Theodoric, son of Ida, reigned 7 years. Freodwald, [son of Ida,] reigned 6 years, and in his time, the kingdom of the Kentishmen received baptism, from the mission of Gregory. Hussa reigned 7 years.

Four kings fought against them, Urien, and Rhydderch Hen, and Gwallawg and Morcant. Theodoric fought vigorously against Urien and his sons. During that time, sometimes the enemy, sometimes the Cymry were victorious, and Urien blockaded them for three days and three nights in the island of Lindisfarne. But during this campaign, Urien was assassinated on the instigation of Morcant, from jealousy, because his military skill and generalship surpassed that of all the other kings.

Aethelferth the Artful reigned 12 years in Bernicia and another 12 in Deira. He reigned 24 years in the two kingdoms, and gave Din Guaire to his wife, whose name was Bebba, and it was named Bamburgh from his wife's name.

Edwin, son of Aelle, reigned 17 years. He occupied Elmet and expelled Ceretic, king of that country. His daughter, Eanfeld, received baptism on the twelfth day after Whitsun, and all his people, men and women, with her. Edwin was baptised at the Easter following, and twelve thousand men were baptised with him. If anyone wants to know who baptised them, †and this is what bishop Renchidus and Elvodug, the holiest of bishops, told me,† Rhun son of Urien, †that is Paulinus, archbishop of York,† baptised them, and for forty days on end he went on baptising the whole nation of the Thugs, and through his teaching many of them believed in Christ.

64.　　　Oswald, son of Aethelferth, reigned for 9 years, and he is Oswald Brightblade. He killed Catwallaun, king of the country of Gwynedd, at the battle of Cantscaul, with a great slaughter of his army.

Oswy, son of Aethelferth, reigned 28 years and 6 months. During his reign came the great plague, and in it died Cadwaladr, who reigned among the British after his father. Oswald killed Penda, at Gaius' Field, and now was the slaughter at Gaius' Field, and the kings of the British, who had gone forth with king Penda in his campaign to the city called Iudeu, were killed.

65.　　　Then Oswy delivered all the riches that he had in the city into the hand of Penda, and Penda distributed them to the kings of the British, that is the 'Distribution of Iudeu'.

But Cadafael, king of the country of Gwynedd, was the only one to escape with his army, by rising up in the night; and so he was called Cadafael the Battle Dodger.

Egferth, son of Oswy, reigned 9 years. In his time, the holy bishop Cuthbert died in the island of Lindisfarne. It was Egferth who made war against the Picts, and fell there.

Penda, son of Pybba, reigned for 10 years. He was the first to separate the kingdom of the Mercians from the kingdom of the Northerners. He treacherously killed Anna, king of the East Angles, and saint Oswald, king of the Northerners. He fought the battle of Cogwy, in which fell his brother, Eobba, son of Pybba, and Oswald, king of the Northerners, and he was victorious through the arts of the Devil; for he was not baptised, and never believed in God.

66.   From the beginning of the world to (the consulship of) Constantinus and Rufus (A.D. 457) are 5,658 years.

Also, from the (consulship of the) Two Twins (Gemini), Fufius and Rubellius, (A.D. 29) to (the consulship of) Stilicho (A.D. 400), 373 years.

And from the (beginning of the) reign of Vortigern to the quarrel between Vitalinus and Ambrosius are 12 years, that is Wallop, the battle of Wallop. Vortigern, however, held empire in Britain in the consulship of Theodosius and Valentinian (A.D. 425), and in the fourth year of his reign the English came to Britain, in the consulship of Felix and Taurus (A.D. 428), in the 400th year from the (Passion) of Our Lord Jesus Christ.

From the year when the English came to Britain and were welcomed by Vortigern to (the consulship of) Decius and Valerian are 69 years (= A.D. 497).

[THE WELSH ANNALS . . . P. 44]

[Welsh Genealogies . . . see *Arthurian Period Sources,* Section G B]

[THE CITIES OF BRITAIN]

66a. These are the names of all the Cities in the whole of Britain, 28 in number.

1. Vortigern's Fortress.	11. Manchester?	20. Caerleon
2. Winchester.	12. London.	21. Caerwent.
3. ??Verulamium??	13. Canterbury.	22. Dumbarton.
4. Carlisle.	14. Canterbury?	23. Leicester?
5. Lindisfarne.	15. Llanberis?	24. Draithou Fortress.
6. ??Colchester??	16. Doncaster.	25. Penselwood Fortress.
7. York.	17. Chester.	26. Urnarc Fortress.
8. Constantine's Fortress.	18. Wroxeter.	27. Celimion Fortress.
9. Caradoc's Fortress.	19. Caernarfon.	28. Wall-by-Lichfield.
10.Cambridge.		

[THE WONDERS OF BRITAIN]

67. The first wonder is Loch Leven. In it are sixty islands, and men live there, and it is surrounded by sixty rocks, and there is an eagle's nest on each rock, and sixty rivers flow into it, and only one river flows from it to the sea, called the Leven.

The second wonder is the estuary of the river Trahannon, for it reaches the shore in a single wave, like a hill, in the Bore, and ebbs like other seas.

The third wonder is the Hot Lake, *where the Baths of Badon are,* in the country of the Hwicce. It is surrounded by a wall, made of brick and stone, and men may go there to bathe at any time, and every man can have the kind of bath he likes. If he wants, it will be a cold bath; and if he wants a hot bath, it will be hot.

68. The fourth wonder is the salt springs found there, from which salt is boiled, wherewith various foods can be salted; they are not near the sea, but rise from the ground.

Another wonder is *Dau Ri Hafren*, that is, the Two Kings of the Severn. When the sea floods into the Severn estuary in the Bore, two heaped-up wave crests are built up separately, and fight each other like rams. One goes against the other, and they clash in turn, and then one withdraws from the other, and they go forth again at each tide. This they have done, from the beginning of the world to the present day.

69. Another wonder is the mouth of Llyn Lliwan. Its estuary is in the Severn, and when the Severn is flooded in the Bore and the sea also floods up the estuary of the aforesaid river, the river is received into the estuary waters like

a whirlpool, and the sea does not go up; and there is a shore by the river, and whenever the Severn is flooded in the Bore, that shore is not touched, and when the sea ebbs from the Severn, then Lake Lliwan spews up everything that is devoured from the sea, and that shore is touched, and, like a hill, breaks and spews up in one wave. And if the army of the whole country where it is should be there, and should front the wave, the force of the wave would drag down the army, its clothing filled with water, and the horses would also be dragged down. But if the army should turn its back on the wave, the wave does not harm it, and when the sea ebbs, then the whole of the shore that the wave covered is laid bare again, and the sea ebbs from it.

70.   There is another wonder in the country of Cynllibiwg. There is a spring there called the Fount of Gorheli. No stream flows into it, or from it. Men go to fish in the spring. Some go to the east of the spring, and take fish thence, and others go to the south, to the north and the west, and draw fish from each part. But different kinds of fish are taken from all parts. It is wonderful that fish are found in the spring, though no river flows into it or from it, and four kinds of fish are found in it, though it is of no great size or depth. It is as deep as a knee, twenty feet in length and breadth, and it has high banks on each side.

By the river called Wye, apples are found on an ash-tree, on the hillside by the river estuary.

There is another wonder in the country called Gwent. There is a cleft, from which the wind always continuously blows. And when there is no wind, in the summer time, it still blows continuously from that cleft, so that no-one can stand in front of the depth of the cleft. In British, it is called by the name of Chwyth Gwynt, in Latin, Windblow. It is a great wonder that wind blows from the earth.

71.   There is another wonder in Gower, the altar in the place called Llwynarth, that is suspended by the will of God. It seems to me better to tell the story of that altar, than to suppress it. For it came to pass that when saint Illtud was praying in a cave by the sea that washes the land at this place, for the mouth of the cave is on the sea, a ship sailed to him from the sea, and two men sailed it, and the body of a holy man was with them in the ship, and an altar was above his face, hanging there by the will of God. The man of God went to meet them, and (saw?) the body of the holy man and the altar stayed inseparably above the face of the holy body. They said to saint Illtud 'This man of God told us to bring him to you and to bury him with you, and you shall not reveal his name to any man, so that men should not swear by him'. So they buried him, and after the burial the two men went back to the ship and sailed away. But saint Illtud built a church about the body of the holy man and about the altar, and the altar remains to this day suspended by the will of God.

41

A local king once came to test it, carrying a stick in his hands. He bent the stick round the altar, and held its two ends in his hands, and pulled it towards him, to test the truth of the matter. But did not live out a full month thereafter. Another man peeped under the altar, and lost the sight of his eyes, and ended his life within the month.

72. There is another wonder in the aforesaid country, called Gwent. There is a spring by the wall of Pydew Meurig, and there is a plank in the middle of the spring, and men may wash their hands and their faces, and have the plank under their feet when they wash. I have tested it and seen it myself. When the sea floods at high tide, the Severn spreads over the whole shore, and touches it, and reaches to the spring, and the spring is filled from the Severn Bore, it draws the plank with it to the open sea, and it is cast about in the sea for three days, but on the fourth day it is found in the same spring. Now it came to pass that a countryman buried it in the ground to test it, and on the fourth day it was found in the spring, and the country-man who took it and buried it died before the end of the month.

73. There is another wonder in the country called Builth. There is a heap of stones there, and one of the stones placed on top of the pile has the foot-print of a dog on it. When he hunted Twrch Trwyth Cafal, the warrior Arthur's hound, impressed his footprint on the stone, and Arthur later brought together the pile of stones, under the stone in which was his dog's footprint, and it is called Carn Cafal. Men come and take the stone in their hands for the space of a day and a night, and on the morrow it is found upon the stone pile.

There is another wonder in the country called Ergyng. There is a tomb there by a spring, called Llygad Amr; the name of the man who is buried in the tomb was Amr. He was a son of the warrior Arthur, and he killed him there and buried him. Men come to measure the tomb, and it is sometimes six feet long, sometimes nine, sometimes twelve, sometimes fifteen. At whatever measure you measure it on one occasion, you never find it again of the same measure, and I have tried it myself.

74. There is another wonder in the country called Ceredigion. There is a mountain there called Crug Mawr, and a tomb on the top of it, and who-ever comes to the tomb and lies beside it, however short he is, the tomb is found to be the same length as the man. If he be a short small man the tomb is found to be as long as the man, and if he be a long tall man, even if he were four cubits long, the tomb is found to be as long as the man. And every traveller who is weary, if he kneels three times before it, he will never be worried by weariness again to the day of his death, even if he should go by himself to the ends of the earth.

42

[THE WONDERS OF MONA]

75.   The first wonder is the shore without a sea. The second wonder is the hill there that turns about itself thrice a year. The third wonder is the ford there. When the sea floods, it is flooded; when the sea ebbs, it dwindles. The fourth wonder is the stone that walks by night in the Vale of Citheinn and was once hurled in the whirlpool of Ceris, that is the midst of the sea called Menai, and on the morrow it was certainly found on the bank of the aforesaid valley.

[THE WONDERS OF IRELAND]

There is a lake there called Loch. Lein. Four circles are around it. In the first circle it is surrounded by tin, in the second by lead, in the third by iron, in the fourth by copper, and in the lake many pearls are found, that kings place in their ears.

There is another lake which hardens wood to stone. Men take wood, and after they have shaped it, they throw it in the lake, and it stays there to the end of the year, and at the end of the year it is found to be stone. It is called Loch Echach.

THE WELSH ANNALS

(*Annales Cambriae*)

The earliest version of the *Welsh Annals* is entered in *Harleian* MS 3859 at the end of *Nennius*, after Chapter 66; but, unlike the rest of the additional matter, it is not reproduced in later editions of *Nennius*, though two later versions are transcribed in other MSS.

The *Harleian* MS is laid out in narrow columns. A complete cycle (see *Nennius* 16) of 532 years plus one is written out, each year beginning a new line, marked as 'an(nus)', and every tenth year numbered. Years L and LX are both noted a year too early, while a year too many is accidentally added to the decades beginning CLX, CCXX, CCL, CCLXXX, CCCXL and CCCLX. There are no entries against most of the first years or the last 33, and many other years are also blank.

Reckoning backwards from the numerous known dates of later centuries, the 533 years should extend from 444 to 977, and modern editors have inserted these dates, in arabic numerals. They are here retained, for purposes of reference, though it is probable the cycle was intended to begin in 447 rather than 444.

Additional entries and detail contained in MS 'B', and absent from the Harleian text, are added between dagger symbols thus † . . . †, with one entry from MS 'C' in double daggers.

J. M.

44

The Welsh Annals

447 Days as dark as night.†

453 Easter altered on the Lord's Day by Pope Leo, Bishop of Rome.

454 St. Brigid is born.

457 St. Patrick goes to the Lord [*i.e. dies*].

458 †St. David is born in the thirtieth year after Patrick left Meneviat.

468 The death of Bishop Benignus.

501 Bishop Ebur rests in Christ [*i.e. dies*], he was 350 years old.

516 The Battle of Badon, in which Arthur carried the Cross of our Lord Jesus Christ for three days and three nights on his shoulders [*i.e. shield*] and the Britons were the victors.

521 St. Columba is born. The death of St. Brigid.

537 The battle of Camlann, in which Arthur and Medraut fell: and there was plague in Britain and Ireland.

544 The sleep [*i.e. death*] of Ciaran.

547 A great death [*i.e. plague*] in which Maelgwn, king of Gwynedd died. †Thus they say 'The long sleep of Maelgwn in the court of Rhos'. Then was the yellow plague.†

558 The death of Gabrán, son of Dungart.

562 Columba went to Britain.

565 †The voyage of Gildas to Ireland†.

569 †The 'Synod of Victory' was held between the Britons†.

570 Gildas †wisest of Britons† died.

573 The battle of Arfderydd †between the sons of Eliffer and Gwenddolau son of Ceidio; in which battle Gwenddolau fell; Merlin went mad.†

574 The sleep [*i.e. death*] of Brendan of Birr.

580 Gwrgi and Peredur †sons of Elifert† died.

584 Battle against the Isle of Man and the burial of Daniel of the Bangors.

589 The conversion of Constantine to the Lord.

594 †Aethelbert reigned in England†.

595 The death of Columba.
The death of king Dunod †son of Pabo.†
Augustine and Mellitus converted the English to Christ.

601 The synod of Urbs Legionis [*i.e. Chester*].
Gregory died in Christ.
and also bishop David of Moni Iudeorum.
606 The burial of bishop Cynog.
607 The death of Aidan son of Gabrán.
612 The death of Kentigern and bishop Dyfrig.
613 The battle of Caer Legion [*i.e. Chester*].
and there died Selyf son of Cynan. And Iago son of Beli slept
[*i.e. died*].
616 Ceredig died.
617 Edwin begins his reign.
624 The sun is covered [*i.e. eclipsed*].
626 Edwin is baptized, and Rhun son of Urien baptized him.
627 Belin dies.
629 The beseiging of king Cadwallon in the island of Glannauc.
630 Gwyddgar comes and does not return.
On the Kalends of January the battle of Meigen; and there Edwin
was killed with his two sons; but Cadwallon was the victor.
631 The battle of Cantscaul [*Denisburna, near Hexham*] in which
Cadwallon fell.
632 The slaughter of the [*river*] Severn and the death of Idris.
644 The battle of Cogfry in which Oswald king of the Northmen and
Eawa king of the Mercians fell.
645 The hammering of the region of Dyfed, when the monastery of
David was burnt.
649 †Slaughter in Gwent†.
650 The rising of a star.
656 The slaughter of Campus Gaius.
657 Penda killed.
658 Oswy came and took plunder.
661 Cummine the tall [*died*].
662 Brocmail †the tusked† dies.
665 The first celebration of Easter among the Saxons. The second
battle of Badon. Morgan dies.
669 Oswy, king of the Saxons, dies.
676 A star of marvellous brightness was seen shining throughout the
whole world.
682 A great plague in Britain, in which Cadwaladr son of Cadwallon dies.
683 A plague †wast† in Ireland.
684 A great earthquake in the Isle of Man.
689 The rain turned to blood in Britain, and †in Ireland† milk and
butter turned to blood.
704 Aldfrith king of the Saxons died.
The sleep [*i.e. death*] of Adomnán.

714 Night was as bright as day. Pepin the elder [*actually Pepin II, of Heristal*], king of the Franks, died in Christ.

717 Osred king of the Saxons dies.

718 The consecration of the church of the archangel Michael †on mount Garganot†.

721 A hot summer.

722 Beli son of Elffin dies. And the battle of Hehil among the Cornish, the battle of Garth Maelog, the battle of Pencon among the south Britons, and the Britons were the victors in those three battles.

728 The battle of mount Carno.

735 Bede the priest sleeps [*i.e. dies*].

736 Oengus king of the Picts died.

750 Battle between the Picts and the Britons, that is the battle of Mocetauc. And their king Talorgan is killed by the Britons. Tewdwr son of Beli dies.

754 Rhodri king of the Britons dies.

757 Ethelbald king of the Saxons dies.

760 A battle between the Britons and the Saxons, that is the battle of Hereford and Dyfnwal son of Tewdwr dies.

768 Easter is changed among the Britons †on the Lord's day† Elfoddw, servant of God, emending it.

775 Ffernfael son of Ithael dies.

776 Cinaed [*Kenneth*] king of the Picts dies.

777 Abbot Cuthbert dies.

778 The devastation of the South Britons by Offa.

784 The devastation of Britain by Offa in the summer.

796 †Devastation by Rheinwg son of Offa† The first coming of the gentiles [*i.e. Norsemen*] among the southern Irish.

797 Offa king of the Mercians and Maredudd king of the Demetians die, and the battle of Rhuddlan.

798 Caradog king of Gwynedd is killed by the Saxons.

807 Arthen king of Ceredigion dies. †Solar eclipse.†

808 Rhain king of the Demetians and Cadell † king † of Powys die.

809 Elfoddw archbishop in the Gwynedd region went to the Lord [*i.e. died*].

810 †The moon covered [*i.e. eclipsed*] †. Mynyw burnt. †Death of cattle in Britain.†

811 Owain son of Maredudd dies.

812 The fortress of Degannwy is struck by lightning and burnt.

813 Battle between Hywel †and Cynan. Hywel† was the victor.

814 There was great thunder and it caused many fires. Tryffin son of Rhain died. And Gruffydd son of Cyngen is killed by treachery by his brother Elisedd after an interval of two months. Hywel

triumphed over the island of Mona and he drove Cynan from there with a great loss of his own army.

816 Hywel was again expelled from Mona † and Cynan †. Cynan the king dies. †Saxons invaded the mountains of Eryri [*i.e. Snowdonia*] and the kingdom of Rhufoniog †.

817 The battle of Llan-faes.

818 †Cenwulf devastated the Dyfed region.†

822 The fortress of Degannwy is destroyed by the Saxons and they took the kingdom of Powys into their own control.

825 Hywel dies.

831 †Lunar eclipse†. Laudent died and Sadyrnfyw Hael of Mynyw died.

840 Nobis the bishop ruled Mynyw.

842 Idwallon dies.

844 Merfyn dies. The battle of Cetill.

848 The battle of Ffinnant. Ithael king of Gwent was killed by the men of Brycheiniog.

849 Meurig was killed by Saxons.

850 Cynin is killed by the gentiles [*i.e. Norsemen*].

853 Mona †is† laid waste by black gentiles [*i.e. Norsemen*].

854 Cynan king of Powys died in Rome.

856 Kenneth king of the Picts died. And Jonathan prince [*i.e. Abbot*] of Abergele dies.

860 †Mael Sechnaill died.†

862 Catgueithen was expelled.

864 Duda laid Glywysing waste.

865 Cian of Nanhyfer died.

866 The city of York was laid waste, that is the battle with the black gentiles [*i.e. Norsemen*].

869 The battle of Bryn Onnen.

870 The fortress of Alt Clud was broken by the gentiles [*i.e. Norsemen*].

871 Gwgon king of Ceredigion was drowned.

873 Nobis †the bishop† and Meurig die.
The battle of Bannguolou.

874 †Llunferth the bishop consecrated†.

875 Dungarth king of Cernyw †that is of the Cornish† was drowned.

876 The battle of Sunday in Mona.

877 Rhodri and his son Gwriad is killed by the Saxons.

878 Aed son of Neill dies.

880 The battle of Conwy. Vengeance for Rhodri at God's hand. †The battle of Cynan.†

882 Catgueithen died.

885 Hywel died in Rome.

887 Cerball died.

889 Suibne the wisest of the Irish died.

892 Hyfaidd dies.
894 Anarawd came with the Angles and laid waste Ceredigion and Ystrad Tywi.
895 The Northmen came and laid waste Lloegr and Bycheiniog and Gwent and Gwynllywiog.
896 †Bread failed in Ireland. Vermin like moles with two teeth fell from the air and ate everything up; they were driven out by fasting and prayer.†
898 †Athelstan king of the Saxons died.†
900 Alfred king of the Gewissi dies.
902 Igmund came to Mona and took Maes Osfeilion.
903 †Merfyn son of Rhodri died and † Llywarch son of Hyfaidd dies.
904 Rhodri † son of Hyfaidd † was beheaded in Arwystli.
906 The battle of Dinmeir and Mynyw was broken.
907 †Bishop † Gorchywyl dies † and king Cormac†.
908 †Bishop † Asser died.
909 King Cadell son of Rhodri dies.
913 Ohter comes † to Britain†.
915 Anarawd king † of the Britons † dies.
917 Queen Aethelflaed died.
919 King Clydog was killed.
921 The battle of Dinas Newydd.
928 Hywel journeyed to Rome. †Helen died†.
935 †Gruffydd son of Owain died.†
938 The battle of Brune [i.e. Brunanburgh].
939 Hyfaidd son of Clydog, and Meurig, died.
941 Aethelstan † king of the Saxons † died.
942 King Afloeg dies.
943 Cadell son of Arthfael was poisoned. And Idwal †son of Rhodri† and his son Elisedd are killed by the Saxons.
944 Llunferth bishop in Mynyw died.
945 †Bishop Morlais died.†
946 Cyngen son of Elisedd was poisoned. And Eneuris bishop in Mynyw died. And Strathclyde was laid waste by the Saxons.
947 Edmund king of the Saxons was killed.
950 Hywel king of the Britons † called the Good † died.
951 And Cadwgan son of Owain is killed by the Saxons. And the battle of Carno †between the sons of Hywel and the sons of Idwal†.
952 †Iago and Idwal the sons of Idwal laid Dyfed waste.†
954 Rhodri son of Hywel dies.

† HISTORIA BRITTONUM †

†a Nennio Sapiente composita †

† Incipiunt / Exberta / [Excerptal / fii / [Run filius] Urbagen de
libro Sancti Germani inventa et origine et genelogia Britonum †

† PRAEFATIO †

†Ego Nennius Sancti Elbodugi discipulus aliqua excerpta scribere curavi,
quae hebitudo gentis Britanniae deiecerat, quia nullam peritiam
habuerunt neque ullam commemorationem in libris posuerunt doctores illius insulae Britanniae. Ego autem coacervavi omne quod inveni
tam de annalibus Romanorum quam de cronicis sanctorum patrum, et
de scriptis Scottorum Saxonumque et ex traditione veterum nostrorum. Quod multi doctores atque librarii scribere temptaverunt, nescio
quo pacto difficilius reliquerunt, an propter mortalitates frequentiss-
imas vel clades creberrimas bellorum. Rogo, ut omnis lector, qui
legerit hunc librum, det veniam mihi, qui ausus sum post tantos haec
tanta scribere quasi garrula avis vel quasi quidam invalidus arbiter.
Cedo illi, qui plus noverit in ista peritia satis quam ego.†

† CAPITULA †

† De Aetatibus Mundi †

†i
1-6

De sex aetatibus mundi, et quot annos unaquaeque tenet.

ii
7-9

Unde dicta sit Britannia, et a quo sit sic nominata, qualiterque
sita, et quot in longum et transversum miliaria habet, quotque
civitates in se continet, quot genera hominum intra se sustinet,
quotque adiacentes insulas possidet, quibus praestantioribus
fluminibus interluitur, per quae divitias et delicias exterorum
regnorum deferuntur.

iii
10

Quod Britones impleverunt eam a mari usque ad mare, et a quo
tempore secundum annales Romanorum inhabitari cepit, qualiterque Romanorum sugillatio, quod in nos iniuste extorquent,
refelli potest, de ortu etiam Bruti et proavorum eius, et quid
magus de eo necdum nato praedixerit.

50

xxvi
28

Quo tempore Britones iugum Romanorum abiecerunt, et quando
Nicena sinodus, Ambrosius, Martinus, Ieronymus floruerunt, et
de Maximiano tyranno et filio eius Victore, qualiter et ubi
interfecti fuerunt. Et quot anni ab initio mundi et ab incarnatione Christi usque ad illud tempus transierunt.

xxvii
30

Quot vicibus Britones Romanorum duces occiderunt, et qua
calliditate eos tamen semper ad auxilia sibi ferenda provocaver-
unt, et quot anni Britones sub dominio Romanorum fuerunt.

xxviii
31

Quod ab expulsione Romanorum usque ad adventum Saxonum,
per annos videlicet XL, tota Britannia sub maximo metu fuit, et
quando Gortigernus rex impius regnavit, quot timoribus quant-
isque anxietatibus oppressus exstitit, quoto anno a passione
domini Saxones suscepit et insulam Tanet ad inhabitandum
tradidit, et de prosapia etiam Hengisti, et quomodo Britanniam
venit, et quod imperium Romanorum super Britones tunc
omnino esse desiit.

xxix
32

Quando sanctus Germanus fidem praedicaturus Britanniam
venerit, et Pelagianam haeresim extirpavit, dampnavit et omnino
destruxit.

xxx
32

De Benli rege infideli et tiranno, qui sanctum Germanum recip-
ere noluit sed aditum domus suae prohibuerit.

xxxi
32

De servo, qui eum ad hospicium invitavit, et de vitulo nocte
occiso, cocto et commesto, et mane coram matre vivo, sano et
integro invento.

xxxii
33

De quodam viro ab eo baptizato et iuxta eius vaticinium mox
defuncto et ab angelo dei suscepto.

xxxiii
34

Qualiter hospitis sui filios de opido educi praecepit et nocte ipsa
arcem cum rege ignis de coelo funditus consumpsit.

xxxiv
35

Quomodo vir ille, qui sanctum hospicio recepit, credidit et baptizatus fuit, et iuxta verbum eius de servo rex factus est de regno
Powisorum, et omnes filios eius post eum.

xxxv
36

Qualiter Britones annonas Saxonibus promiserunt, ut pro eis
adversus hostes, scilicet Pictos et Scottos dimicarent, sed postea
facere noluerunt.

54

De mirabilibus Britannice insule

(De mirabilibus Monae insulae)

De mirabilibus Hibernie

Expliciunt capitula

58

1 A principio mundi usque ad diluvium anni II CC XL II.
A diluvio usque ad Abraham anni D CCCC XL II.
Ab Abraham usque ad Moysen anni D C XL.
A Moyse usque ad David anni D.

2 A David usque Nabuchodonosor anni sunt D LX VIIII.
Ab Adam usque transmigrationem Babyloniae anni sunt IIII DCCC
LXX VIIII.
3 A transmigratione Babyloniae usque ad Christum D LX VI.
Ab Adam vero usque ad passionem Christi anni sunt V CC XX VIII.

4 A passione autem Christi peracti sunt anni D CC LXXXX VI.
Ab incarnatione autem eius anni sunt D CCC XXX I.

5 Prima igitur aetas mundi ab Adam usque ad Noe.
Secunda a Noe usque ad Abraham.
Tertia ab Abraham usque ad David.
Quarta aetas a David usque ad Danielem.
Quinta aetas a Daniele usque ad Johannem Baptistam.
Sexta a Johanne usque ad iudicium, in quo dominus noster Iesus
Christus veniet iudicare vivos ac mortuos et seculum per ignem.

7 Brittania insula a quodam Bruto, consule Romano, dicta.
Haec consurgit ab Africo boreali ad occidentem versus. D CCC in
longitudine milium, CC in latitudine spatium habet. In ea sunt viginti
octo civitates et innumerabilia promuntoria cum innumeris castellis
ex lapidibus et latere fabricatis, et in ea habitant quattuor gentes:
Scotti, Picti, Saxones atque Brittones.

8 Tres magnas insulas habet, quarum una vergit contra Armoricas et
vocatur Inis Gueith; secunda sita est in umbilico maris inter Hiberniam
et Britanniam, et vocatur nomen eius Eubonia, id est Manau; alia sita
est in extremo limite orbis Brittanniae, ultra Pictos, et vocatur Orc.
Sic in proverbio antiquo dicitur, quando de iudicibus vel regibus
sermo fuit: 'Iudicavit Brittanniam cum tribus insulis.'

9   Sunt in ea multa flumina, quae confluunt ad omnes partes, id est ad
orientem, ad occidentem, ad meridiem, ad septentrionem, sed tamen
duo flumina praeclariora ceteris fluminibus, Tamesis ac Sabrinae,
quasi duo brachia Britanniae, per quae olim rates vehebantur ad
portandas divitias pro causa negotiationis. Brittones olim implentes
eam a mari usque ad mare iudicaverunt.

10   Si quis scire voluerit quo tempore post diluvium habitata est haec
insula, hoc experimentum bifarie inveni.
   In annalibus autem Romanorum sic scriptum est. Aeneas post
Troianum bellum cum Ascanio filio suo venit ad Italiam et, superato
Turno, accepit Laviniam, filiam Latini, filii Fauni, filii Saturni, in
coniugium et, post mortem Latini, regnum obtinuit Romanorum vel
Latinorum. Aeneas autem Albam condidit et postea uxorem duxit, et
peperit ei filium nomine Silvium. Silvius autem duxit uxorem, et
gravida fuit, et nuntiatum est Aeneae quod nurus sua gravida esset, et
misit ad Ascanium filium suum, ut mitteret magum suum ad consid-
erandam uxorem, ut exploraret quid haberet in utero, si masculum
vel feminam. Et magus consideravit uxorem et reversus est. Propter
hanc vaticinationem magus occisus est ab Ascanio, quia dixit
Ascanio quod masculum haberet in utero mulier et filius mortis erit,
quia occidet patrem suum et matrem suam et erit exosus omnibus
hominibus. Sic evenit: in nativitate illius mulier mortua est, et nutritus
est filius, et vocatum est nomen eius Britto. Post multum intervallum,
iuxta vaticinationem magi, dum ipse ludebat cum aliis, ictu sagittae
occidit patrem suum, non de industria, sed casu. Et expulsus est ab
Italia, et arminilis fuit, et venit ad insulas maris Tirreni, et expulsus
est a Graecis causa occisionis Turni, quem Aeneas occiderat, et
pervenit ad Gallos usque, et ibi condidit civitatem Turonorum, quae
vocatur Turnis. Et postea ad istam pervenit insulam, quae a nomine
suo accepit nomen, id est Brittaniam, et inplevit eam cum suo genere,
et habitavit ibi. Ab illo autem die habitata est Brittannia usque in
hodiernum diem.

† Haec est genealogia istius Bruti exosi, nunquam ad se, nos id est Britones,
ducti, quandoque volebant Scotti, nescientes originis sui, ad istum domari.

† Brutus vero fuit filius Silvii f. Aschanii f. Enee f. Anchise f. Capen
f. Asaraci f. Tros f. Erectonii f. Dardani filii Iupiter, de genere Cam filii
maledicti videntis et ridentis patrem Noe. Tros vero duos filios habuit,
Hilium Asaracumque. Hilius condidit Hilium civitatem, id est Troiam,
primo, genuitque Lamedon. Ipse est pater Priami. Asaracus autem genuit
Capen. Ipse est pater Anchise. Anchises genuit Eneam. Ipse Eneas pater
Ascanii. †

† Is amlaid sin tugasdair ar senoir-ne uasal, i. Guanach, geinilach Breatan a cronicib na Romanach. †

† Sic inveni, ut tibi, Samuel, id est infans magistri mei, id est Beulani presbyteri, in ista pagina scripsi. Set haec genealogia non scripta in aliquo volumine Britanniae, set in scriptione mentis scriptoris fuit. †

11 Aeneas autem regnavit tribus annis apud Latinos. Ascanius regnavit annis XXXVII. Post quem Silvius, Aeneae filius, regnavit annis XII, Postumus annis XXXIX. A quo Albanorum reges Silvii appellati sunt. Cuius frater erat Britto.

Quando regnabat Britto in Brittannia, Heli sacerdos iudicabat in Israhel, et tunc arca testamenti ab alienigenis possidebatur, Postumus, frater, eius, apud Latinos regnabat.

12 Post intervallum multorum annorum, non minus octingentorum Picti venerunt et occupaverunt insulas quae vocantur Orcades, et postea ex insulis vastaverunt regiones multas, et occupaverunt eas in sinistrali plaga Brittanniae, et manent ibi usque in hodiernum diem. Tertiam partem Brittaniae tenuerunt et tenent usque in hodiernum diem.

13 Novissime autem Scotti venerunt a partibus Hispaniae ad Hiberniam. Primus autem venit Partolomus cum mille hominibus, de viris et mulieribus, et creverunt usque ad quattuor milia hominum, et venit martalitas super eos, et in una septimana omnes perierunt et non remansit ex illis etiam unus. Secundus venit ad Hiberniam Nimeth, filius quidam Agnominis, qui fertur navigasse super mare annum et postea tenuit portum in Hibernia, fractis navibus ejus, et mansit ibidem per multos annos, et iterum navigavit cum suis, et ad Hispaniam reversus est. Et postea venerunt tres filii militis Hispaniae cum triginta ciulis apud illos et cum triginta conjugibus in unaquaque ciula et manserunt ibi per spatium unius anni. Et postea conspiciunt turrim vitream in medio mare, et homines conspiciebant super turrim, et quaerebant loqui ad illos, nunquam respondebant, et ipsi uno anno ad oppugnationem turris properaverunt cum omnibus ciulis suis et cum omnibus mulieribus, excepta una aiula, quae confracta est naufragio, in qua erant viri triginta totidemque mulieres. Et aliae naves navigaverunt ad expugnandam turrim, et, dum omnes descenderent in litore, quod erat circa turrim, operuit illos mare, et demersi sunt, et non evasit unus ex illis. Et de familia illius ciulae, quae relicta est propter fractionem, tota Hibernia impleta est usque in hodiernum diem. Et postea venerunt paulatim a partibus Hispaniae et tenuerunt regiones plurimas.

† Nulla tamen certa historia originis Scottorum reperitur. †

14 Novissime venit Damhoctor et ibi habitavit cum omni genere usque hodie in Brittaniam. Istoreth, Istorini filius, tenuit Dalrieta cum suis; Builc autem cum suis tenuit Euboniam insulam et alias circiter; filii autemLiethan obtinuerunt in regione Demetorum †ubi civitas est quae vocatur Mineut·et in aliis regionibus, id est Guir Cetgueli, donec expulsi sunt a Cuneda et a filius eius ab omnibus Brittannicis regionibus.

15 Si quis autem scire voluerit quando vel quo tempore fuit inhabitabilis et deserta Hibernia, sic mihi peritissimi Scottorum nuntiaverunt. Quando venerunt per Mare Rubrum filii Israhel, Aegyptii venerunt, et secuti sunt et demersi sunt, ut in Lege legitur. Erat vir nobilis de Scythia cum magna familia apud Aegyptios, et expulsus est a regno suo, et ibi erat quando Aegyptii mersi sunt, et non perrexit ad sequendum populum Dei. Illi autem qui superfuerant inierunt consilium ut expellerent illum, ne regnum illorum obsideret et occuparet, quia fortes illorum demersi erant in Rubrum mare, † iste gener Pharaonis erat, id est mas Scotte, filie Pharaonis, a quo ut fertur Scocia appellata fuit † et expulsus est. At ille, per XLII annos ambulavit per Africam, et venerunt ad aras Filistinorum et per lacum Salinarum, et cenerunt inter Rusicadam at montes Azariae, et venerunt per flumen Malvam, et transierunt per Maritaniam ad columnas Erculis, et navigaverunt Tyrrenum mare, et pervenerunt ad Hispaniam usque, et ibi habitaverunt per multos annos, et creverunt et multiplicati sunt nimis, et gens illorum multiplicata est nimis. Et postea venerunt ad Hiberniam post MII annos, postquam mersi sunt Aegyptii in Rubrum mare, et ad regiones Darieta, in tempore quo regnabat Brutus apud Romanos, a quo consules esse coeperunt, deinde tribuni plebis ac dictatores. Et consules rursum rempublicam obtinuerunt per annos CCCCXLVII, quae prius regia dignitate damnata fuerat.

Brittones venerunt in tertia aetate mundi ad Brittaniam; Scotti autem in quarta obtinuerunt Hiberniam. Scotti autem, qui sunt in occidente, et Picti de aquilone pugnabant unanimiter et uno impetu contra Brittones indesinenter, quia sine armis utebantur Brittones. Et post multum intervallum temporis Romani monarchiam totius mundi obtinuerunt.

16 A primo anno, quo Saxones venerunt in Brittanniam, usque ad annum quartum Mermini regis, supputantur anni CCCCXXVIIII. A nativitate Domini usque ad adventum Patricii ad Scottos, CCCCV anni sunt. A morte Patricii usque ad obitum sanctae Brigidae, LX anni. A nativitate Columbae usque mortem Brigidae, IV anni sunt.

Initium compoti: XXIII cycli decemnovenales ab incarnatione Domini usque ad adventum Patricii in Hiberniam, et ipsi annos efficiunt numero CCCCXXXVIII, et ab adventu Patricii usque ad cyclum decemnovenalem, in quo sumus, XXII cycli sunt, id est CCCCXXI sunt, II anni, in ogdoade usque in hunc annum, in quo sumus.

17 Aliud experimentum inveni de isto Bruto ex veteribus libris veterum nostrorum.
    Tres filii Noe diviserunt orbem in tres partes post diluvium. Sem in Asia, Cham in Africa, Jafeth in Europa dilataverunt terminos suos. Primus homo venit ad Europam de genere Jafeth Alanus cum tribus filiis suis, quorum nomina sunt Hessitio, Armeno, Negue. Hessitio autem habuit filios quattuor: hi sunt Francus, Romanus, Britto, Albanus. Armenon autem habuit quinque filios: Gothus, Valagothus, Gebidus, Burgundus. Negue autem habuit tres filios: Wandalus, Saxo, Boguarus. Ab Hisitione autem ortae sunt quattuor gentes: Franci, Latini, Albani et Britti. Ab Armenone autem quinque: Gothi, Walagothi, Gebidi, Burgundi, Langobardi. A Neguio vero quattuor: Boguarii, Vandali, Saxones et Turingi. Istae autem gentes subdivisae sunt per totam Europam. Alanus autem, ut aiunt, filius fuit Fetebir, filii Ougomun, filii Thoi, filii Boib, filii Simeon, filii Mair, filii † Ethach, filii. † Aurthach, filii † Ecthet, filii. † Oth, filii Abir, filii Rea, filii Ezra, filii Izrau, filii Baath, filii Iobaath, filii Jovan, filii Jafeth, filii Noe, filii Lamech, filii Matusalem, filii Enoch, filii Jareth, filii Malaleel, filii Cainan, filii Enos, filii Seth, filii Adam, filii Dei vivi. Hanc peritiam inveni ex traditione veterum.

18 Qui incolae in primo fuerunt Brittanniae. Brittones a Bruto. Brutus filius Hisitionis, Hisition Alanei; Alaneus filius Reae Silviae; Rea Silvia filia Numae Pampilii, filii Ascanii; Ascanius filius Aeneae, filii Anchisae, filii Troi, filii Dardani, filii Flise, filii Juvani, filii Jafeth. Jafeth vero habuit septem filios. Primus Gomer, [a quo Galli; secundus Magog, a quo Scythas et Gothos; tertius Madai], a quo Medos; quartus Juvan, a quo Graeci; quintus Tubal, a quo † Hiberei † et Hispani et Itali; sextus Mosoch, a quo Cappadoces; septimus Tiras, a quo Traces. Hi sunt filii Jafeth, filii Noe, filii Lamech.

[de Brittannia Romana]

19 Et redeam nunc ad id de quo digressus sum.
    Romani autem, dum acciperent dominium totius mundi, ad Brittannos miserunt legatos, ut obsides et censum acciperent ab illis, sicut accipiebant ab universis regionibus et insulis. Brittanni autem, cum essent tyranni et tumidi, legationem Romanorum contempserunt. Tunc Julius Caesar, cum accepisset singulare imperium primus et obtinuisset, iratus, est valde, et venit ad Brittanniam cum sexaginta ciulis, et tenuit in ostium Tamesis, in quo naufragium perpessae sunt naves illius, dum ipse pugnabat apud Dolobellum, qui erat proconsul regi Brittannico, qui et ipse Bellinus

vocabatur, et filius erat Minocanni, qui occupavit omnes insulas Tyrreni maris, et Julius reversus est sine victoria, caesis militibus et fractis navibus.

20 Et iterum, post spatium trium annorum, venit cum magno exercitu trecentisque ciulis, et pervenit usque ad ostium fluminis, quod vocatur Tamesis. Et ibi inierunt bellum et multi ceciderunt de equis militibusque suis, quia supradictus proconsul posuerat sudes ferreos et semen bellicosum, id est cetilou, in vada fluminis. Discrimen magnum fuit militibus Romanorum haec ars invisibilis et discesserunt sine pace in illa vice. Gestum est bellum tertio juxta locum qui dicitur Trinovantum.

Et accepit Julius imperium Brittannicae gentis XLVII annis ante nativitatem Christi, ab initio autem mundi VCCXV.

Julius igitur primus in Brittanniam pervenit, et regnum et gentem tenuit, et in honorem illius Quintilem mensem Julium debere Romani decreverunt vocari. Et idibus Martiis Gaius Julius Caesar in curia occiditur, tenente Octaviano Augusto monarchiam totius mundi, et censum a Brittannia ipse solus accepit, ut Virgilius ait

Purpurea intexti tollant aulaea Brittanni.

21 Secundus post hunc Claudius imperator venit, et in Brittannia imperavit annis XLVIII post adventum Christi, et stragem et bellum fecit magnum non absque detrimento militum, tamen victor fuit in Brittannia. Et postea cum ciulis perrexit ad Orcades insulas, et subjecit sibi, et fecit eas tributarias. In tempore illius quievit dare censum Romanis a Brittannia, sed Brittannicis imperatoribus redditum est. Regnavit annis XIII, mensibus VIII. Cujus monumentum in Mogantia apud Longobardos ostenditur: dum ad Romam ibat, ibi defunctus est.

22 Post CLXVII annos post adventum Christi Lucius, Brittannicus rex, cum omnibus regulis totius Brittannicae gentis, baptismum suscepit, missa legatione ab imperatoribus Romanorum et a papa romano Eucharisto.

23 Tertius fuit Severus, qui transfretavit ad Brittanos; ubi, ut receptas provincias ab incursione barbarica faceret tutiores, murum et aggerem a mari usque ad mare per latitudinem Brittanniae, id est CXXXII milia passuum deduxit, et vocatur brittannico sermone Guaul. † id est a Penguaul, quae villa scotice Cenail, anglice vero Peneltun dicitur, usque ad ostium fluminis Cluth et Cair Pentaloch, quo murus ille finitur. Rustico opere Severus ille praedictus construxit, set nihil profuit. Carutius postea imperator reedificavit et VII castellis munivit inter utraque ostia, domumque rotundam politis lapidibus super ripam fluminis Carun, quod a suo nomine nomen accepit, fornicem triumphalem in victoriae memoriam erigens construxit. † Propterea

jussit fieri inter Brittones et Pictos et Scottos, quia Scotti ab occidente et
Picti ab aquilone unanimiter pugnabant contra Brittones, nam et ipsi pacem
inter se habebant; et non multo post intra Brittanniam Severus moritur.
† intra Britanniam reversus apud Eboracum cum suis ducibus occiditur. †

24 Quartus fuit Karitius imperator et tyrannus, qui et ipse in Brittanniam
venit tyrannide. Qui propterea tyrannus fuit pro occisione Severi et cum
omnibus ducibus romanicae gentis, qui erant cum eo in Brittannia,
transverberavit omnes regulos Brittannorum et vindicavit valde Severum
ab illis et purpuram Brittanniae occupavit.

25 Quintus Constantinus, Constantini magni filius, fuit, et ibi moritur, et
sepulchrum illius monstratur juxta urbem quae vocatur Cair Segeint, ut
litterae, quae sunt in lapide tumuli, ostendunt. Et ipse seminavit tria
semina, id est auri, argenti aerisque, in pavimento supradictae civitatis, ut
nullus pauper in ea habitaret unquam, et vocatur alio nomine Minmanton.

26 Sextus Maximus imperator regnavit in Brittania. A tempore illius consules
esse coeperunt et Caesares nunquam appellati sunt postea. Et sanctus
Martinus in tempore illius claruit in virtutibus et signis, et cum eo locutus est.

27 Septimus imperator regnavit in Brittannia Maximianus. Ipse perrexit cum
omnibus militibus Brittonnum a Brittannia, et occidit Gratianum, regem
Romanorum, et imperium tenuit totius Europae, et noluit dimittere milites,
qui perrexerunt cum eo, ad Brittanniam, ad uxores suas et ad filios suos et
ad possessiones suas, sed dedit illis multas regiones a stagno quod est super
verticem Montis Jovis usque ad civitatem quae vocatur Cant Guic, et usque
ad cumulum occidentalem, id est Cruc Ochident. † Britones namque
Armorici, qui ultra mare sunt, cum Maximo tyranno hinc in expeditionem
exiuntes, quoniam redire nequiverant, occidentales partes Galliae solo
tenus vastaverunt, nec mingentes ad parietem vivere reliquerunt, acceptisque
eorum uxoribus et filiabus in coniugium omnes earum linguas amputaverunt,
ne eorum successio maternam linguam disceret; unde et nos illos vocamus
in nostra lingua Letewicion, id est semitacentes, quoniam confuse
loquuntur. † Hi sunt Brittones Armorici, et nunquam reversi sunt hucusque
in hodiernum diem. Propter hoc Brittannia occupata est ab extraneis
gentibus et cives expulsi sunt, usque dum Deus auxilium dederit illis.
[*Britonibus in Brittania imperator ultimus praefuit.*]
    In veteri traditione seniorum nostrorum septem imperatores fuerunt a
Romanis in Brittannia, Romani autem dicunt novem. Octavus fuit alius
Severus, qui aliquando in Brittannia manebat, aliquando ad Romam ibat
et ibi defunctus est. Nonus fuit Constantius. Ipse regnavit XVI annis in
Brittannia et in sextodecimo anno imperii sui obiit in Brittannia.

28 Hucusque regnaverunt Romani apud Brittones CCCCVIIII annis. Brittones autem dejecerunt regnum Romanorum neque censum dederunt illis neque reges illorum acceperunt, ut regnarent super eos, neque Romani ausi sunt ut venirent Brittanniam ad regnandum amplius, quia duces illorum Brittones occiderant.

29 Iterum repetendus est sermo de Maximiano tyranno. Gratianus cum fratre Valentiniano regnavit VI annis, et Ambrosius Mediolanensis episcopus clarus habetur in catholicorum dogmate. Valentinianus cum Theodosio regnavit annis VIII. Synodus Constantinopolim colligitur a CCCXVIII patribus, in qua omnes haereses damnantur. Hieronymus tum presbyter Bethleem toto mundo claruit. Dum Gratianus imperium regebat in toto mundo, in Brittannia per seditionem militum Maximus imperator factus est. Qui mox dum in Gallias transfretaret, Gratianus Parisiis Merobaudis, magistri militum, proditione superatus est et fugiens Lugduni captus atque occisus est. Maximus Victorem, filium suum, consortem fecit. Martinus, Turonensis episcopus, in magnis virtutibus claruit. Post multum intervallum temporis a Valentiniano et Theodosio consulibus in tertio ab Avvileua lapide spoliatus indumentis regiis sistitur et capite damnatur. Cujus filius Victor eodem anno ab Arbogaste comite interfectus est in Gallia.

30 Tribus vicibus occisi sunt duces Romanorum a Brittannis.
    Brittones autem dum anxiebantur a barbarorum gentibus, id est Scottorum et Pictorum, flagitabant auxilium Romanorum, et, dum legati mittebantur, cum magno luctu et cum sablonibus super capita sua intrabant, et portabant magna munera secum consulibus Romanorum pro admisso scelere occisionis ducum, et suscipiebant consules grata dona ab illis, et promittebant cum juramento accipere jugum Romanici juris, licet durum fuisset.
    Et Romani venerunt cum maximo exercitu ad auxilium eorum et posuerunt imperatores in Brittannia et composito imperatore cum ducibus revertebantur exercitus ad Romam usque, et sic alternatim per CCCXLVIII annos faciebant. Brittones autem propter gravitatem imperii occidebant duces Romanorum et auxilium postea petebant. Romani autem ad imperium auxiliumque et ad vindicandum veniebant et, spoliata Brittannia auro argentoque cum aere et omni pretiosa veste et melle, cum magno triumpho revertebantur.

[de rebus postea gestis]
[in Cantia, I]

31 Factum est autem post supradictum bellum, id est quod fuit inter Brittones et Romanos, quando duces illorum occisi sunt, et occisionem

Maximi tyranni, transactoque Romanorum imperio in Brittannis, per XL annos fuerunt sub metu. Guorthigirnus regnavit in Brittannia, et dum ipse regnabat in Brittannia, urgebatur a metu Pictorum Scottorumque et a Romanico impetu, nec non et a timore Ambrosii. Interea venerunt tres ciulae a Germania expulsae in exilio, in quibus erant Hors et Hengist, qui et ipsi fratres erant, filii Guictglis, filii Guitta, filii Guectha, filii Woden, filii Frealaf, filii Fredulf, filii Finn, filii Fodepald, filii Geta, qui fuit, ut aiunt, filius Dei: non ipse est Deus deorum, amen, Deus exercituum, sed unus est ab idolis eorum, quod ipsi colebant. Guorthigirnus suscepit eos benigne et tradidit eis insulam quae in lingua eorum vocatur Tanet, britannico sermone Ruoihm.

Regnante Gratiano secundo cum Equitio, Saxones a Guorthigirno suscepti sunt, anno CCCXLVII post passionem Christi.

† Et in tempore Guorthigirni, regis Britanie, Saxones pervenerunt in Britanniam, id est in anno Incarnacionis Christi [. . .], sicut [S] libine ab [b] as Iae in Ripum civitate invenit vel reperit, ab Incarnacione Domini anni D usque ad kl. Jan. in XII luna; ut aiunt alii, intis CCC annis a quo tenuerunt Saxones Britanniam usque ad supradictum. †

[a Sancto Germano, I]

32 In tempore illius venit sanctus Germanus ad praedicandum in Brittania, et claruit apud illos in multis virtutibus, et multi per eum salvi facti sunt et plurimi perierunt.

Aliquanta miracula, quae per illum fecit Deus, scribenda decrevi.

Primum miraculum de miraculis ejus.

Erat quidam rex iniquus atque tyrannus valde, cui nomen erat Benli. Illum vir sanctus voluit visitare et properare ad iniquum regem, ut praedicaret illi. At cum ipse homo Dei venisset ad ostium urbis cum comitibus suis, venit portarius et salutavit eos, et miserunt eum ad regem, et rex durum responsum dedit illis et cum juramento dixit: 'Si fuerint vel si manserint usque ad caput anni, non venient unquam in medio urbis meae.' Dum ipsi expectarent januatorem, ut nuntiaret illis sermonem tyranni, dies declinabat ad vesperum, et nox appropinquabat, et nescierunt quo irent. Interea venit unus de servis regis e medio urbis, et inclinavit se ante virum Dei, et nuntiavit illis omnia verba tyranni, et invitavit illos ad casam suam, et exierunt cum eo, et benigne suscepit eos. Et ille nihil habebat de omnibus generibus jumentorum, excepta una vacca cum vitulo, et occidit vitulum, et coxit, et posuit ante illos. Et praecepit sanctus Germanus ut non confringeretur os de ossibus ejus, et sic factum est, et in crastino vitulus inventus est ante matrem suam sanus et vivus incolumisque.

33 Iterum de mane surrexerunt, ut impetrarent salutationem tyranni. At ipsi cum orarent et expectarent juxta portam arcis, et ecce vir unus currebat, et sudor illius a vertice ad plantas pedum distillabat. Inclinabat se ante illos, et dixit sanctus Germanus: 'Credis in Sanctam Trinitatem?' Et respondit illis: 'Credo', et baptizatus est, et osculavit eum, et dixit illi: 'Vade in pace: in ista hora morieris, et angeli Dei in aere expectant te, ut gradieris cum illis ad Deum, cui credidisti.' Et ipse laetus intravit in arcem, et praefectus tenuit illum, et alligavit, et ante tyrannum ductus interfectus est, quia mos erat apud nequissimum tyrannum, nisi quis ante solis ortum pervenisset ad servitutem in arce, interficiebatur. Et manserunt tota die juxta portam civitatis, et non impetraverunt ut salutarent tyrannum.

34 Solito ex more supradictus affuit servus, et dixit illi sanctus Germanus: 'Cave ne unus homo maneat de hominibus tuis in ista nocte in arce.' Et ipse reversus est in arcem, et deduxit filios suos, quorum numerus erat novem, et ipsi ad supradictum hospitium cum ipso reversi sunt Et praecepit sanctus Germanus manere eos jejunos et clausis januis dixit: 'Vigilantes estote, et si quid evenerit in arce, nolite aspicere, sed orate indesinenter et ad Deum vestrum clamate.' Et post modicum intervallum noctis ignis de caelo cecidit, et combussit arcem et omnes homines qui cum tyranno erant, et nusquam apparuerunt usque in hodiernum diem, et arx non aedificata est usque hodie.

35 In crastino die ille vir, qui hospitalis fuit illis, credidit et baptizatus est cum omnibus filiis suis et omnis regio cum eis: cui nomen erat Catel. Et benedixit ei, et addidit, et dixit: 'Non deficiet rex de semine tuo † in aeterunum †. Ipse est Catell Durnluc, et tu solus rex eris ab hodierna die.' Et sic evenit, et impletum est quod dictum est per prophetam dicentem: 'Suscitans de pulvere egenum, et de stercore erigens pauperem, ut sedeat cum principibus et solium gloriae teneat.' Juxta verba sancti Germani rex de servo factus est, et omnes filii ejus reges facti sunt, et a semine illorum omnis regio Povisorum regitur usque in hodiernum diem.

[in Cantia II]

36 Factum est autem, postquam metati sunt Saxones in supra dicta insula Tanet, promisit rex supradictus dari illis victum et vestimentum absque defectione; et placuit illis, et ipsi promiserunt expugnare inimicos ejus fortiter. At illi barbari cum multiplicati essent numero, non potuerunt Brittones cibare illos. Cum postularent cibum et vestimentum, sicut promissum erat illis, dixerunt Brittones: 'Non possumus dare vobis cibum et vestimentum, quia numerus vester multiplicatus est, sed recedite a nobis,

68

quia auxilio vestro non indigemus.' Et ipsi consilium fecerunt cum majoribus suis, ut pacem disrumperent.

37 Hencgistus autem, cum esset vir doctus atque astutus et callidus, cum explorasset super regem inertem et super gentem illius, quae sine armis utebatur, inito consilio, dixit ad regem Brittannicum: 'Pauci sumus; si vis, mittemus ad patriam nostram ac invitemus milites de militibus nostrae regionis, ut amplior sit numerus ad certandum pro te et pro gente tua.' Et ille imperavit ut facerent, et miserunt, et legati transfretaverunt trans Tithicam vallem, et reversi sunt cum ciulis sedecim, et milites electi venerunt in illis, et in una ciula ex eis venit puella pulchra facie atque decorosa valde, filia Hencgisti. Postquam autem venissent ciulae, fecit Hencgistus convivium Guorthigirno et militibus suis et interpreti suo, qui vocabatur Ceretic, et puellam jussit ministrare illis vinum et siceram, et inebriati sunt et saturati sunt nimis. Illis autem bibentibus, intravit Satanas in corde Guorthigirni, ut amaret puellam, et postulavit eam a patre suo per interpretem suum et dixit: 'Omne quod postulas a me impetrabis, licet dimidium regni mei.' Et Hencgistus, inito consilio cum suis senioribus, qui venerunt secum de insula Oghgul, quid peterent regi pro puella, unum consilium cum illis omnibus fuit ut peterent regionem quae in lingua eorum vocatur Canturguoralen, in nostra autem Chent. Et dedit illis, Guoyrancgono regnante in Cantia, et inscius erat quia regnum ipsius tradebatur paganis et ipse solus in potestatem illorum clam dari, et sic data est puella illi in conjugium, et dormivit cum ea, et amavit eam valde.

38 Et dixit Hencgistus ad Guorthigirnum: 'Ego sum pater tuus et consiliator tui ero, et noli praeterire consilium meum umquam, quia non timebis te superari ab ullo homine neque ab ulla gente, quia gens mea valida est. Invitabo filium meum cum fratrueli suo, bellatores enim viri sunt, ut dimicent contra Scottos, et da illis regiones quae sunt in aquilone, juxta murum qui vocatur Guaul.' Et jussit ut invitaret eos, et invitavit Octha et Ebissa cum quadraginta ciulis. At ipsi cum navigarent circa Pictos, vastaverunt Orcades insulas, et venerunt, et occupaverunt regiones plurimas ultra mare Frenessicum, usque ad confinium Pictorum. Et Hencgistus semper ciulas ad se paulatim invitavit, ita ut insulas ad quas venerant absque habitatore relinquerent, et dum gens illius crevisset et in virtute et in multitudine, venerunt ad supradictum civitatem Cantorum.

39 Nam, super omnia mala adjiciens, Guorthigirnus accepit filiam sui uxorem sibi, et peperit ei filium. Et hoc cum compertum esset a sancto Germano, eum corripere venit cum omni clero Brittonum. Et dum conventa esset magna synodus clericorum ac laicorum in uno concilio, ipse rex praemonuit filiam suam ut exiret ad conventum et ut daret filium suum in sinum Germani et ut diceret quod ipse erat pater filii; et mulier fecit sicut erat edocta. Germanus autem eum benigne accepit et dicere coepit: 'Pater tibi ero nec te dimittam, nisi mihi novacula cum forcipe pectineque detur et ad patrem tuum carnalem tibi dare licetur.' Et obaudivit puer, et usque ad avum suum patrem carnalem Guorthigirnum perrexit, et puer illi dixit: 'Pater meus es, caput meum tonde et comam capitis mei.' Et ille siluit, et tacuit; et puero respondere noluit, sed surrexit et iratus est valde, ut a facie sancti Germani fugeret, et maledictus est, et damnatus a sancto Germano et omni Brittonum concilio.

[de Ambrosio]

40 Et postea rex ad se invitavit magos suos, ut quid faceret ab eis interrogaret. At illi dixere: 'In extremas fines regni tui vade, et arcem munitam invenies, ut te defendas, quia gens quam suscepisti in regno tuo invidet tibi, et te per dolum occidet, et universas regiones quas amaras occupabit cum tua universa gente post mortem tuam'. Et postea ipse cum magis suis arcem adipisci venit, et per multas regiones multasque provincias circumdederunt et, illis non invenientibus, ad regionem quae vocatur Guined novissime pervenerunt; et, illo lustrante in montibus Hereri, † id est Snaudun anglice, † tandem in uno montium loco, in quo aptum erat arcem condere, adeptus est. Et magi ad illum dixere: 'Arcem in isto loco fac, quia tutissima a barbaris gentibus in aeternum erit.' Et ipse artifices congregavit, id est lapidicinos, et ligna et lapides congregavit et, cum esset congregata omnis materia, in una nocte ablata est materia. Et tribus vicibus jussit congregari, et nusquam comparuit. Et magos arcessivit, et illos percunctatus est, quae esset haec causa malitiae et quid hoc eveniret. At illi responderunt: 'Nisi infantem sine patre invenies, et occidetur ille, et arx a sanguine suo aspergatur, numquam aedificabitur in aeternum.'

41 Et ipse legatos ex consilio magorum per universam Brittanniam misit, utrum infantem sine patre invenirent. Et, lustrando omnes provincias regionesque plurimas, venerunt ad campum Elleti, qui est in regione quae vocatur Gleguissing, et pilae ludum faciebant pueri. Et ecce duo inter se

litigabant, et dixit alter alteri: 'O homo sine patre, bonum non habebis.'
At illi de puero ad pueros diligenter percunctabantur, et cunctantes matrem,
si patrem haberet. Illa negavit et dixit: 'Nescio quomodo in utero meo con-
ceptus est, sed unum scio quia virum non cognovi umquam'; et juravit illis
patrem non habere. Et illi eum secum duxere usque ad Guorthigirnum
regem et eum insinuaverunt regi.

42 Et in crastino conventio facta est, ut puer interficeretur. Et puer ad regem
dixit: ['Cur viri tui me ad te detulerunt?' Cui rex ait: 'Ut interficiaris, et
sanguis tuus circa arcem istam aspergetur, ut possit aedificari.' Respondit
puer regi:] 'Quis tibi monstravit?' Et respondit rex: 'Magi mei mihi dixere.'
Et puer dixit: 'Ad me vocentur.' Et invitati sunt magi et puer illis dixit:
'Quis revelavit vobis ut ista arx a sanguine meo aspergeretur et, nisi aspergeretur a sanguine meo, in aeternum non aedificabitur? Sed hoc ut cognos-
catis, quis mihi de me palam fecit?' Iterum puer dixit: 'Modo tibi, o rex,
elucubrabo et in veritate tibi omnia satagam; sed magos tuos percunctor:
quid in pavimento istius loci est? Placet mihi ut ostendant tibi quid sub
pavimento habetur.' At illi dixere: 'Nescimus.' Et ille dixit: 'Comperior:
stagnum in medio pavimenti est; venite et fodite, et sic invenietis.'
Venerunt, et foderunt, et ruit. Et puer ad magos dixit: 'Proferte mihi, quid
est in stagno?' Et siluerunt et non potuerunt revelare illi. Et ille dixit illis:
'Ego vobis revelabo: duo vasa sunt et sic invenietis.' Venerunt et viderunt
sic. Et puer ad magos dixit: 'Quid in vasis conclusis habetur?' At ipsi siluerunt et non potuerunt revelare illi. At ille asseruit: 'In medio eorum tentorium est, separate ea et sic invenietis.' Et rex separari jussit, et sic inventum
est tentorium complicatum, sicut dixerat. Et iterum interrogavit magos
ejus: 'Quid in medio tentorii est? Etiam nunc narrate.' Et non potuerunt
scire. At ille revelavit: 'Duo vermes in eo sunt, unus albus et alter rufus;
tentorium expandite.' Et extenderunt et duo vermes dormientes inventi
sunt. Et dixit puer: 'Expectate et considerate quid facient vermes.' Et
coeperunt vermes ut alter alterum expelleret; alius autem scapulas suas
ponebat, ut eum usque ad dimidium tentorii expelleret; et sic faciebant
tribus vicibus: tandem infirmior videbatur vermis rufus, et postea fortior
albo fuit, et extra finem tentorii expulit; tunc alter alterum secutus trans
stagnum est, et tentorium evanuit. Et puer ad magos refert: 'Quid significat
mirabile hoc signum quod factum est in tentorio?' Et illi proferunt:
'Nescimus.' Et puer respondit: 'En revelatum est mihi hoc mysterium, et
ego vobis propalabo. Regni tui figura tentorium est; duo vermes duo
dracones sunt; vermis rufus draco tuus est; et stagnum figura hujus mundi
est. At ille albus draco illius gentis, quae occupavit gentes et regiones plurimas in Brittannia, et paene a mari usque ad mare tenebunt, et postea gens
nostra surget, et gentem Anglorum trans mare viriliter deiciet. Tu tamen
de ista arce vade, quia eam aedificare non potes, et multas provincias cir-

71

cumi, ut arcem tutam invenias, et ego hic manebo.' Et rex ad adolescentem
dixit: 'Quo nomine vocaris?' Ille respondit: 'Ambrosius vocor', id est
Embreis Guletic ipse videbatur. Et rex dixit: 'De qua progenie ortus es?'
Et ille: 'Unus est pater meus de consulibus romanicae gentis.' Et arcem
dedit rex illi cum omnibus regnis occidentalis plagae Brittanniae, et ipse
cum magis suis ad sinistralem plagam pervenit et usque ad regionem quae
vocatur Guunnessi affuit, et urbem ibi, quae vocatur suo nomine Cair
Guorthigirn, aedificavit.

[in Cantia, III]

43 Interea Guorthemir, filius Guorthigirn, cum Hengisto et Horso et cum
gente illorum petulanter pugnabat et eos usque ad supradictam insulam,
quae vocatur Tanet, expulit et eos ibi tribus vicibus conclusit, obsedit, per-
cussit, comminuit, terruit. Et ipse legatos ultra mare usque in Germaniam
transmittebant vocando ciulas cum ingenti numero bellatorum virorum.
Et postea pugnabant contra reges nostrae gentis: alliquando vincebant
et dilatabant terminos suos, aliquando vincebentur et expellebantur.

44 Et Guorthemir contra illos quattuor bella avide gessit. Primum bellum super
flumen Derguentid; secundum bellum super vadum quod dicitur in lingua
eorum Episford, in nostra autem lingua Rithergabail, et ibi cecidit Hors
cum filio Guorthigirni, cujus nomen erat Categirn; tertium bellum in campo
juxta Lapidem tituli, qui est super ripam Gallici maris, commisit, et barbari
victi sunt, et ille victor fuit, et ipsi in fugam versi usque ad ciulas suas mersi
sunt in eas muliebriter intrantes. Ille autem post modicum intervallum
mortuus est et ante mortem suam ad familiam suam dixit ut sepulchrum
illius in portu ponerent a quo exierant, super ripam maris, 'in quo vobis
commendo: quamvis in alia parte portum Brittanniae teneant et habitaver-
int, tamen in ista terra in aeternum non manebunt.' Illi autem mandatum
ejus contempserunt et eum in loco in quo imperaverat illis non sepelierunt.
† In Lincolnia enim sepultus est. At si mandatum eius tenuissent, procul
dubio per orationes sacti Germani quicquid pecierant obtinuissent. †

45 At barbari reversi sunt magno opere, cum Guorthigirnus amicus eis erat
propter uxorem suam, et nullus illos abigere audaciter valuit, quia non de
virtute sua Brittanniam occupaverunt, sed de nutu Dei. Contra voluntatem
Dei quis resistere poterit et nitatus? Sed quomodo voluit Dominus fecit et
ipse omnes gentes regit et gubernat.

Factum est autem post mortem Guorthemir, regis Guorthigirni filii, et
post reversionem Hengisti cum suis turbis, consilium fallax hortati sunt, ut
dolum Guorthigirno cum exercitu suo facerent. At illi legatos, ut impetra-

72

rent pacem, miserunt, ut perpetua amicitia inter illos fieret. At ille Guorthegirnus cum suis majoribus natu [consilium fecerunt et scrutati sunt quid facerent. Tandem unum] consilium cum omnibus fuit, ut pacem facerent, et legati eorum reversi sunt, et postea conventum adduxerunt, ut ex utraque parte Brittones et Saxones in unum sine armis convenirent, ut firma amicitia esset.

46 Et Hengistus omni familiae suae jussit ut unusquisque artavum suum sub pede in medio ficonis sui poneret: 'Et quando clamavero ad vos et dixero *Eu, nimet saxas!*, cultellos vestros ex ficonibus vestris educite, et in illos irruite, et fortiter contra illos resistite. Et regem illorum nolite occidere, sed eum, pro causa filiae meae, quam dedi illi in conjugium, tenete, quia melius est nobis ut ex manibus nostris redimatur.' Et conventum adduxerunt, et in unum convenerunt, et Saxones, amicialiter locuti, in mente interim vulpicino more agebant, et vir juxta virum socialiter sederunt. Hengistus, sicut dixerat, vociferatus est, et omnes seniores trecenti Guorthigirni regis jugulati sunt, et ipse solus captus, et catenatus est, et regiones plurimas pro redemptione animae suae illis tribuit, id est Est saxum, Sutsaxum, † Middelseaxan cum reliquis regionibus quas ipsi eligentes nominaverunt. †

[a Sancto Germano, III]

47 Sanctus vero Germanus Guorthigirno praedicabat ut ad Dominum suum converteret et ab illicita conjunctione se separaret; et ille usque ad regionem quae a nomine suo accepit nomen Guorthigirniaun miserabiliter effugit, ut ibi cum uxoribus suis lateret. Et sanctus Germanus post illum secutus est cum omni clero Brittonum, et ibi quadraginta diebus et quadraginta noctibus mansit, et super petram et die orabat noctuque stabat. Et iterum Guorthigirnus usque ad Arcem Guorthigirni, quae est in regione Demetorum, juxta flumen Teibi, ignominiose abcessit. Et solito more sanctus Germanus eum secutus est, et ibi jejunus cum omni clero tribus diebus totidemque noctibus causaliter mansit, et in quarta nocte arx tota mediae circa noctis horam per ignem missum de caelo ex improviso cecidit, ardente igne caelesti; et Guorthigirnus cum omnibus qui cum eo erant et cum uxoribus suis defecit. Hic est finis Guorthigirni, ut in Libro beati Germani repperi. Alii autem aliter dixerunt.

48 Postquam exosi fuerunt illi † propter susceptionem populi Saxonici † omnes homines gentis suae pro piaculo suo inter potentes et impotentes, inter servum et liberum, inter monachos et laicos, inter parvum et magnum, et ipse dum de loco ad locum vagus errat, tandem cor ejus crepuit et

73

defunctus est, non cum laude. Alii dixerunt: terra aperta est et deglutivit eum in nocte in qua combusta est arx circa eum, quia non inventae sunt ullae reliquiae illorum qui combusti sunt cum eo in arce.

Tres filios habuit, quorum nomina sunt Guorthemir, qui pugnabat contra barbaros, ut supra diximus, secundus Categirn, tertius Pascent, qui regnavit in duabus regionibus Buelt et Guorthegirniaun post mortem patris sui, largiente Ambrosio illi, qui fuit rex † magnus † inter omnes reges Brittannicae gentis. Quartus fuit Faustus, qui a filia sua genitus est illi, et sanctus Germanus baptizavit illum, et nutrivit, et docuit, et condidit locum magnum super ripam fluminis quod vocatur Renis, et manet usque hodie. Et unam filiam habuit, quae fuit mater Fausti sancti.

49 Haec est genealogia illius, quae ad initium retro recurrit. Fernmail ipse est, qui regit modo in regionibus duabus Buelt et Guorthigirniaun filius Teudubir. Teudubir ipse est rex Buelitiae regionis, filius Pascent filii Guoidcant, filii Moriud, filii Eldat, filii Edoc, filii Paul, filii Mepurit, filii Briacat, filii Pascent, filius Guorthigirn Guortheneu, filius Guitaul, filii Guitolin, filii Gloiu. Bonus, Paul, Mauron, Guotolin, quattuor fratres fuerunt filii Gloiu, qui aedificavit urbem magnam super ripam fluminis Sabrinae, quae vocatur brittannico sermone Cair Gloiu, saxonice autem Gloecester. Satis dictum est de Guorthigirno et de genere suo.

50 Sanctus Germanus reversus est post mortem illius ad patriam suam.

[de Sancto Patricio]

Et Sanctus Patricius erat in illo tempore captivus apud Scottos, et dominus illius nominabatur Milchu, et porcarius cum illo erat, et in septimo decimo anno aetatis suae reversus est de captivitate, et nutu Dei eruditus est postea in sacris litteris, et ad Romam usque pervenit, et per longum spatium mansit ibidem. Ad legendum et ad scrutanda mysteria Dei et sanctarum scripturarum libros percurrit. Nam cum ibi esset per annos septem, missus est Palladius episcopus primitus a Caelestino episcopo et papa Romae ad Scottos in Christum convertendos; sed prohibuit illum Deus per quasdam tempestates, quia nemo potest accipere quicquam de terra, nisi de caelo datum fuerit illi desuper. Et profectus est ille Palladius de Hibernia, et pervenit ad Brittanniam, et ibi defunctus est in terra Pictorum.

51 Audita morte Palladii eipiscopi, alius legatus Patricius, Theodosio et Valentiano regnantibus, a Caelestino papa romano et angelo Dei, cui nomen erat Victor, monente et suadente sancto Germano episcopo, ad

Scottos in fidem Christi convertendos mittitur. Misit Germanus seniorem cum illo Segerum ad quendam hominem mirabilem summum episcopum Amatheam regem in propinquo habitantem. Ibi sanctus sciens omnia quae ventura essent illi, episcopalem gradum Amatheo rege episcopus sanctus accepit, et nomen quod est Patricius sumpsit, quia prius Maun vocabatur. Auxilius et Iserinus et ceteri inferiori gradu simul ordinati sunt cum eo.

52 Tunc, acceptis benedictionibus perfectisque omnibus in nomine sanctae Trinitatis, paratam ascendit navim, et pervenit ad Brittanniam, et praedicavit ibi non multis diebus, et amissis omnibus ambulandi anfractibus summa velocitate flatuque prospero mare Hibernicum cum navi descendit. Onerata vero navis cum transmarinis mirabilibus et spiritalibus thesauris perrexit ad Hiberniam, et baptizavit eos.

53 A mundi principio usque ad baptismum Hiberniensium VCCCXXX anni sunt. In quinto anno Loygare regis exorsus est praedicare fidem Christi.

54 Sanctus itaque Patricius evangelium Christi externis nationibus per annos quadraginta praedicabat, virtutes apostolicas faciebat, caecos illuminabat, leprosos mundabat, surdos audire faciebat, daemones ab obsessis corporibus fugiebat, mortuos numero usque ad novem suscitavit, captivos multos utriusque sexus suis propriis donis redemit. Scripsit abegetoria trecenta sexaginta quinque aut eo amplius. Ecclesias quoque eodem numero fundavit trecentas sexaginta quinque. Ordinavit episcopos trecentos sexaginta quinque aut eo amplius, in quibus spiritus Dei erat. Presbyteros autem usque ad tria milia ordinavit, et duodecim milia hominum in una regione Conachta ad fidem Christi convertit et baptizavit, [et septem reges, qui erant filii Amolgith, in uno die baptizavit]. Quadraginta diebus et quadraginta noctibus in cacumine collis Eile jejunavit, id est Cruachan Eile; in quo colle in aere imminente tres petitiones pro his qui fidem ex Hibernensibus receperunt elementer postulavit. Prima petitio ejus est, ut dicunt Scotti, id est ut susciperet unusquisque paenitentiam, licet in extremo vitae suae statu; secunda, ut ne a barbaris consumentur in aeternum; tertia, ut non supervixerit aliquis Hiberniensium in adventu judicii, quia delebuntur pro honore Patricii septem annis ante judicium. In illo autem tumulo benedixit populis Hiberniae, et ideo ascendit, ut oraret pro eis et videret fructum laboris sui. Et venerunt ad eum aves multi coloris innumerabiles, ut benediceret illis, quod significat omnes sanctos utriusque sexus autem Hiberniensium pervenire ad eum in die judicii ad patrem et ad magistrum suum, ut sequantur illum ad judicium. Postea in senectute bona migravit, ubi nunc laetatur in saecula saeculorum. Amen.

55 Quattuor modis aequantur Moyses et Patricius: id est angelo collo-
quente in rubo igneo; secundo modo, in monte quadraginta diebus et
quadraginta noctibus jejunavit; tertio modo, similes fuerunt aetate
CXX annis; quarto modo sepulchrum illius nemo scit, sed in occulto
humatus est, nemine sciente. XV annis in captivitate, in vicesimo
quinto anno ab Amatheo sancto episcopo subrogatur, LXXXV annis
in Hibernia praedicavit. Res autem exigebat amplius loqui de sancto
Patricio, sed tamen pro compendio sermonis volui breviare.

[de Arturo]

56 In illo tempore Saxones invalescebant in multitudine et crescebant in
Brittannia. Mortuo autem Hengisto, Octha, filius ejus, transivit de sinistrali parte Brittanniae ad regnum Cantorum, et de ipso orti sunt reges
Cantorum. Tunc Arthur pugnabat contra illos in illis diebus cum regibus Brittonum, sed ipse dux erat bellorum. Primum bellum fuit in
ostium fluminis quod dicitur Glein. Secundum, et tertium, et quartum,
et quintum super aliud flumen, quod dicitur Dubglas, et est in regione
Linnuis. Sextum bellum super flumen quod vocatur Bassas. Septimum
fuit bellum in silva Celidonis, id est Cat Coit Celidon. Octavum fuit
bellum in castello Guinnion, in quo Arthur portavit imaginem sanctae
Mariae perpetuae virginis super humeros suos, et pagani versi sunt in
fugam in illo die, et caedes magna fuit super illos per virtutem Domini
nostri Jesu Christi et per virtutem sanctae Mariae virginis genitricis ejus.
Nonum bellum gestum est in urbe Legionis. Decimum gessit bellum in
litore fluminis quod vocatur Tribruit. Undecimum factum est bellum
in monte qui dicitur Agned. Duodecimum fuit bellum in monte
Badonis, in quo corruerunt in uno die nongenti sexaginta viri de uno
impetu Arthur; et nemo prostravit eos nisi ipse solus, et in omnibus
bellis victor extitit. Et ipsi, dum in omnibus bellis prosternebantur,
auxilium a Germania petebant, et augebantur multipliciter sine intermissione, et reges a Germania deducebant, ut regnarent super illos in
Brittannia usque ad tempus quo Ida regnavit, qui fuit Eobba filius.
Ipse fuit primus rex in Beornica, id est im Berneich.

[de Nordhumbrensium et Anglorum regibus]

57 Woden genuit Beldeg,
genuit Beornec,
genuit Gechbrond,
genuit Aluson,
genuit Inguec,
genuit Aedibrith,
genuit Ossa,
genuit Eobba,
genuit Ida.
Ida autem duodecim filios habuit, quorum nomina sunt:
Adda, Aedldric, Decdric, Edric, Deothere, Osmer, et unam reginam
Bearnoch, Ealric.
Ealdric genuit Aelfret.
Ipse est Aedlferd Flesaur. Nam et ipse habuit filios septem, quorum
nomina sunt:
Anfrid, Osguald, Osbiu, Osguid, Osgudu, Oslapf, Offa.
Osguid genuit Alcfrid, et Aelfguin, et Echfird.
Echgfrid ipse est qui fecit bellum contra fratruelem suum, qui erat rex
Pictorum, nomine Birdei, et ibi corruit cum omni robore exercitus sui, et
Picti cum rege suo victores extiterunt, et numquam addiderunt Saxones
ambronum ut a Pictis vectigal exigerent. A tempore istius belli vocatur
Gueith Lin Garan.
Osguid autem habuit duas uxores, quarum una vocabatur Rieinmelth,
filia Royth, filii Rum, et altera vocabatur Eanfled, filia Eadguin, filii Alli.

De genealogia regum Cantiae

58 Hengist genuit Octha, genuit Ossa, genuit Eormoric, genuit Ealdbert,
genuit Ealdbald, genuit Ercunbert, genuit Ecgberth.

De ortu regum Estanglorum

59 Woden genuit Casser, genuit Titinon, genuit Trigil, genuit Rodmunt,
genuit Rippan, genuit Guillem Guechan.
Ipse primus regnavit in Brittannia super gentem Estanglorum.
Guecha genuit Guffan, genuit Tydil, genuit Ecni, genuit Edric, genuit
Aldul, genuit Elric.

De genealogia Merciorum

60 Woden genuit Guedolgeat, genuit Gueagon, genuit Guithleg, genuit Guerd-mund, genuit Offa, genuit Ongen, genuit Eamer, genuit Pubba.
Ipse Pubba habuit duodecim filios, quorum duo notitiores mihi sunt quam alii, id est Penda et Eva.
Eadlit filius Pantha, Penda filius Pubba.
Eadbalt filius Alguing, filius Eva, filius Penda, filius Pubba.
Ecgfrid filius Offa, filius Duminfert, filius Eandulf, filius Ossulf, filius Eva, filius Pubba.

De regibus Deurorum

61 Woden genuit Beldeyg. Brond genuit Siggar, genuit Sebald, genuit Zegulf, genuit Soemil.
Ipse primus separavit Deur o Birneich.
Soemil genuit Sguerthing, genuit Giulglis, genuit Usfrean, genuit Iffi, genuit Ulli, Aedgum, Osfird, et Eadfird.
Duo filii Edguin erant, et cum ipso corruerunt in bello Meicen, et de origine illius numquam iteratum est regnum, quia non evasit unus de genere illius de isto bello, sed interfecti omnes sunt cum illo ab exercitu Catguoll-auni, regis Guendotae regionis.
Osguid genuit Ecgfrid. Ipse est Ecgfird Ailguin. Genuit Oslach, genuit Alhun, genuit Adlsing, genuit Echun, genuit Oslaph.
Ida genuit Eadric, genuit Ecgulf, genuit Liodguald, genuit Aetan.
Ipse est Eata Glinmaur.
Genuit Eadbyrth et Ecgbirth episcopum, qui fuit primus de natione eorum.

de numero annorum quibus regnaverunt

Ida, filius Eobba, tenuit regiones in sinistrali parte Brittanniae, id est Umbri maris, et regnavit annis duodecim, et junxit Dinguayrdi guurth Berneich, † quae duae regiones fuerunt in una regione, id est Deura Bernech, anglice Deira et Bernicia. †

62 Tunc Outigirn in illo tempore fortiter dimicabat contra gentem Anglorum.
Tunc Talhaern Tataguen in poemate claruit; et Neirin, et Taliessin, et Bluchbard, et Cian, qui vocatur Gueinth Guaut, simul uno tempore in poemate Brittannico claruerunt.

Mailcunus magnus rex apud Brittones regnabat, id est in regione Guenedotae, quia atavus illius, id est Cunedag, cum filiis suis, quorum numerus
octo erat, venerat prius de parte sinistrali, id est de regione quae vocatur
Manau Guotodin, CXLVI annis antequam Mailcun regnaret, et Scottos cum
ingentissima clade expulerunt ab istis regionibus, et nusquem reversi sunt
iterum ad habitandum.

63 Adda, filius Ida, regnavit annis VIII. Aedlric, filius Adda, regnavit IV annis.
Deoric, filius Ida, regnavit VII annis. Friodolguald regnavit VI annis.
In cujus tempore regnum Cantiorum, mittente Gregorio, baptismum
suscepit.
Hussa regnavit annis VII.
Contra illum quattuor reges, Urbgen, et Riderchhen, et Guallauc, et
Morcant, dimicaverunt. Deodric contra illum Urbgen cum filiis dimicabat
fortiter. In illo autem tempore aliquando hostes, nunc cives vincebantur,
et ipse conclusit eos tribus diebus et tribus noctibus in insula Metcaud et,
dum erat in expeditione, jugulatus est, Morcanto destinante pro invidia,
quia in ipso prae omnibus regibus virtus maxima erat instauratione belli.
Eadfered Flesaurs regnavit XII annis in Berneich et alios XII in Deur;
XXIV annis inter duo regna regnavit, et dedit uxori suae Dinguoaroy, quae
vocatur Bebbab, et de nomine suae uxoris suscepit nomen, id est Bebbanburth.
Edguin, filius Alli, Regnavit annis XVII. Et ipse occupavit Elmet, et expulit
Certic, regem illius regionis. Eanfled, filia illius, duodecimo die post Pente-
costen baptismum accepit cum universis hominibus suis, de viris et mulieribus, cum ea. Eadguin vero in sequenti Pasca baptismum suscepit et duodecim milia hominum baptizati sunt cum eo. Si quis scire voluerit quis eos
baptizavit, † sic mihi Renchidus episcopus et Elbodus episcoporum
sanctissimus tradiderunt, † Rum map Urbgen † , id est Paulinus Ebora-
censis archiepiscopus, † baptizavit eos, et per quadraginta dies non cessavit
baptizare omne genus ambronum et per praedicationem illius multi
crediderunt in Christo.

64 Oswald, filius Eadfred, regnavit IX annis. Ipse est Oswald Lamnguin. Ipse
occidit Catgublaun, regem Guenedotae regionis, in bello Catscaul, cum
magna clade exercitus sui.
Osguid, filius Eadlfrid, regnavit XXVIII annis et VI mensibus. Dum ipse
regnabat, venit mortalitas hominum, Catgualart regnante apud Brittones
post patrem suum, et in ea periit. Et ipse occidit Pantha in campo Gai, et
nunc facta est strages Gai campi, et reges Brittonum interfecti sunt, qui
exierant cum rege Pantha in expeditione usque ad urbem quae vocatur Iudeu.

65 Tunc reddidit Osguid omnes divitias quae erant cum eo in urbe usque in
manu Pendae, et Penda distribuit ea regibus Brittonum, id est Atbret
Iudeu. Solus autem Catgabail, rex Guenedotae regionis, cum exercitu suo

evasit de nocte consurgens: quapropter vocatus est Catgabail Catguommed. Ecgfrid, filius Osbiu, regnavit IX annis. In tempore illius sanctus Cudbertus episcopus obiit in insula Medcaut. Ipse est qui fecit bellum contra Pictos et corruit ibi.

Penda, filius Pybba, regnavit X annis. Ipse primus separavit regnum Merciorum a regno Nordorum, et Onnan, regem Easteranglorum, et sanctum Oswaldum, regem Nordorum, occidit per dolum. Ipse fecit bellum Cocboy, in quo cecidit Eoua, filius Pippa, frater ejus, rex Merciorum, et Oswald, rex Nordorum, et ipse victor fuit per diabolicam artem. Non erat baptizatus et nunquam Deo credidit.

[de Chronographia]

66 A mundi principio usque ad Constantinum et Rufum, $\overline{V}$DCLVIII anni reperiuntur.

Item, a duobus Geminis Rufo et Rubelio usque in Stillitionem consulem, CCCLXXIII anni sunt.

Item, a Stillitione usque ad Valentinianum, filium Placidae, et regnum Guorthigirni, XXVIII anni.

Et a regno Guorthigirni usque ad discordiam Guitolini et Ambrosii anni sunt XII, quod est Guoloppum, id est Catguoloph. Guorthigirnus autem tenuit imperium in Brittannia Theodosio et Valentiniano consulibus, et in quarto anno regni sui Saxones ad Brittanniam venerunt, Felice et Tauro consulibus, CCCC anno ab incarnatione Domini nostri Jesu Christi.

Ab anno quo Saxones venerunt in Brittanniam et a Guorthigirno suscepti sunt usque ad Decium et Valerianum anni sunt LXIX.

[de Civitatibus Brittanniae]

66a Haec sunt nomina omnium civitatum quae sunt in tota Brittannia, quarum numerus est XXVIII.

1. Cair Guorthigirn	11. Cair Maunguid	20. Cair Legeion Guar Usic
2. Cair Guinntguic	12. Cair Lundem	21. Cair Guent
3. Cair Mincip	13. Cair Ceint	22. Cair Brithon
4. Cair Ligualid	14. Cair Guiragon	23. Cair Lerion
5. Cair Meguaid	15. Cair Peris	24. Cair Draitou
6. Cair Colun	16. Cair Daun	25. Cair Pensa vel Coyt
7. Cair Ebrauc	17. Cair Legion	26. Cair Urnarc
8. Cair Custoeint	18. Cair Guricon	27. Cair Celemion
9. Cair Caratauc	19. Cair Segeint	28. Cair Luit Coyt
10. Cair Grauth		

[de Mirabilibus Brittanniae]

67   Primum miraculum est stagnum Lumonoy. In eo sunt insulae sexaginta, et ibi habitant homines, et sexaginta rupibus ambitur, et nidus aquilae in unaquaque rupe est, et flumina fluunt sexaginta in eo, et non vadit ex eo ad mare nisi unum flumen, quod vocatur Lemn.

Secundum miraculum ostium Trahannoni fluminis, quia in una unda instar montis ad sissam tegit litora et recedit ut cetera maria.

Tertium miraculum stagnum calidum *in quo balnea sunt Badonis,* quod est in regione Huich, et muro ambitur ex latere et lapide facto, et in eo vadunt homines per omne tempus ad lavandum, et unicuique, sicut placuerit illi, lavacrum sic fiat sibi secundum voluntatem suam: si voluerit, lavacrum frigidum erit; si calidum, calidum erit.

68   Quartum miraculum est: fontes in eadem inveniuntur de salo, a quibus fontibus sal coquitur; inde diversa cibaria saliuntur et non prope sunt mari, sed de terra emergunt.

Aliud miraculum est Duorig Habren, id est duo reges Sabrinae. Quando inundatur mare ad sissam in ostium Sabrinae, duo cumuli spumarum congregantur separatim et bellum faciunt inter se in modum arietum; et procedit unusquisque ad alterum, et collidunt se ad invicem, et iterum secedit alter ab altero, et iterum procedunt in unaquaque sissa. Hoc faciunt ab initio mundi usque in hodiernum diem.

69   Aliud miraculum est, id est Oper Linn Liuan. Ostium fluminis illius fluit in Sabrina, et quando Sabrina inundatur ad sissam, et mare inundatur similiter in ostio supradicti fluminis et in stagno ostii recipitur in modum voraginis, et mare non vadit sursum, et est litus juxta flumen, et quamdiu Sabrina inundatur ad sissam, istud litus non tegitur, et quando recedit mare et Sabrina, tunc stagnum Liuan eructat omne quod devoravit de mari et litus istud tegitur et instar montis in una unda eructat et rumpit. Et si fuerit exercitus totius regionis, in qua est, et direxerit faciem contra undam, et exercitum trahit unda per vim, humore repletis vestibus, et equi similiter trahuntur. Si autem exercitus terga versus fuerit contra eam, non nocet ei unda, et quando recesserit mare, totum tunc litus quod unda tegit retro denudatur et mare recedit ab ipso.

70   Est aliud mirabile in regione Cinlipiuc. Est ibi fons nomine Finnaun Guur Helic. Non fluit rivus ex eo neque in eo. Vadunt homines piscari ad fontem, alii vadunt in fonte ad partem orientis et deducunt pisces ex ea parte, alii ad dextram, alii ad sinistram ad occidentemque, et trahuntur pisces ab unaquaque parte. Et aliud genus piscium trahitur ex omnibus partibus. Magnum mirabile pisces [inveniri] in fonte, dum non flumen fluit in eo neque ex eo,

81

et in eo inveniuntur quattuor genera piscium et non est de magnitudine neque de profunditate. Profunditas illius usque genua, viginti pedes sunt in longitudine et latitudine, ripas altas habet ex omni parte.

Juxta flumen quod vocatur Guoy, poma inveniuntur super fraxinum in proclivo saltus qui est prope ostio fluminis.

Est aliud mirabile in regione quae vocatur Guent. Est ibi fovea, a qua ventus flat per omne tempus sine intermissione; et quando non flat ventus in tempore aestatis, de illa fovea incessanter flat, ut nemo possit sustinere neque ante foveae profunditatem. Et vocatur nomen ejus Vith Guint brittannico sermone, latine autem flatio venti. Magnum mirabile est ventus de terra flare.

71 Est aliud mirabile in Guhyr altare, quod est in loco qui dicitur Loyngarth, quod nutu Dei fulcitur. Historia istius altaris melius mihi videtur narrare quam reticere. Factum est autem, dum sanctus Iltutus orabat in spelunca quae est juxta mare, quod alluit terram supra dicti loci, os autem speluncae ad mare est, et ecce navis navigabat ad se de mari et duo viri navigantes eam, et corpus sancti hominis erat cum illis in navi et altare supra faciem ejus, quod nutu Dei fulciebatur, et processit homo Dei obviam illis, et corpus sancti hominis et altare inseparabiliter supra faciem sancti corporis stabat. Et dixerunt ad sanctum Iltutum: 'Ille homo Dei commendavit nobis ut deduceremus illum ad te et sepeliremus eum tecum, et nomen ejus non reveles ullo homini, ut non jurent per se homines'. Et sepelierunt eum, et post sepulturam illi duo viri reversi sunt ad navim et navigaverunt. At ille sanctus Iltutus ecclesiam fundavit circa corpus sancti hominis et circa altare et manet usque in hodiernum diem altare nutu Dei fulctum. Venit quidam regulus, ut probaret, portans virgam in manu sua; curvavit eam circa altare, et tenuit ambabus manibus virgam ex utraque parte, et traxit ad se, et sic veritatem illius rei probavit, et ille postea per mensem integrum non vixit. Alter vero sub altare aspexit et aciem oculorum ejus amisit et ante mensem integrum vitam finivit.

72 Est aliud mirabile in supra dicta regione Guent. Est ibi fons juxta vallum putei Mouric et lignum in medio fontis, et lavant homines manus suas cum faciebus suis, et lignum sub pedibus suis habent, quando lavant. Nam et ego probavi et vidi. Quando mare inundatur, ad mallinam extenditur Sabrina super omnem maritimam, et tegit, et usque ad fontem producitur, et impletur fons de sissa Sabrinae, et trahit lignum secum usque ad mare magnum, et per spatium trium dierum in mare invertitur, et in quarto die in supra dicto fonte invenitur. Factum est autem, ut unus de rusticis sepeliret eum in terra ad probandum, et in quarto die inventus est in fonte et ille rusticus, qui eum abscondidit et sepelivit, defunctus est ante finem mensis.

73 Est aliud mirabile in regione quae dicitur Buelt. Est ibi cumulus lapidum et
unus lapis superpositus super congestum cum vestigio canis in eo. Quando
venatus est porcum Troynt, impressit Cabal, qui erat canis Arthuri militis,
vestigium in lapide, et Arthur postea congregavit congestum lapidum sub
lapide, in quo erat vestigium canis sui, et vocatur Carn Cabal. Et veniunt
homines, et tollunt lapidem in manibus suis per spatium diei et noctis, et
in crastino die invenitur super congestum suum.

Est aliud miraculum in regione quae vocatur Ercing. Habetur sepulcrum
juxta fontem, qui cognominatur Licat Amr, et viri nomen: qui sepultus est
in tumulo, sic vocabatur Amr; filius Arthuri militis erat, et ipse occidit eum
ibidem et sepelivit. Et veniunt homines ad mensurandum tumulum in longitudine aliquando sex pedes, aliquando novem, aliquando duodecim, aliquando quindecim. In qua mensura metieris eum in ista vice, iterum non
invenies eum in una mensura, et ego solus probavi.

74 Est aliud mirabile in regione quae vocatur Cereticiaun. Est ibi mons, qui
cognominatur Cruc Maur, et est sepulcrum in cacumine illius, et omnis
homo quicumque venerit ad sepulcrum et extenderit se juxta illud, quamvis brevis fuerit, in una longitudine invenitur sepulcrum et homo, et, si
fuerit homo brevis et parvus, similiter et longitudinem sepulcri juxta staturam hominis invenitur, et, si fuerit longus atque procerus, etiamsi fuisset in
longitudine quattuor cubitorum, juxta staturam uniuscujusque hominis sic
tumulus reperitur. Et omnis peregrinus taediosusque homo tres flectiones
flectaverit juxta illud, non erit super se usque ad diem mortis suae, et non
gravabitur iterum ullo taedio, etiamsi abisset solus in extremis finibus
cosmi.

[de Mirabilibus Monae]

75 Primum miraculum est litus sine mari.

Secundum miraculum est ibi mons qui gyratur tribus vicibus in anno.

Tertium miraculum vadum est ibi. Quando inundatur mare, et ipse inundatur; et quando decrescit mare, et ipse minuitur.

Quartum miraculum est lapis qui ambulat in nocturnis temporibus super
vallem Citheinn, et projectus est olim in voragine Cereuus, qui est in medio
pelagi quod vocatur Mene, et in crastino super ripam supra dictae vallis
inventus est sine dubio.

[de Mirabilibus Hiberniae]

Est ibi stagnum quod vocatur Luchlein. Quattuor circulis ambitur.
Primo circulo gronna stanni ambitur, secundo circulo gronna plumbi ambi-

tur, tertio circulo gronna ferri ambitur, quarto circulo gronna aeris ambitur, et in eo stagno multae margaritae inveniuntur, quas ponunt reges in auribus suis.

Est aliud stagnum qui facit ligna durescere in lapides. Homines autem fingunt ligna et, postquam formaverint, projiciunt in stagno, et manet in eo usque ad caput anni et in capite anni lapis reperitur: et vocatur Luch Echach.

†447 an. Dies tenebrosa sicut nox. †
  an. an. an. an. an. an. an. an.
453 an. Pasca commutatur super diem dominicum cum papa Leone episcopo Romae.
454 an.X Brigida sancta nascitur.
  an. an.
457 an. Sanctus Patricius ad Dominum migratur.
  an. an. an. an. an. an. an.XX an. an. an.
†458 an. S. Dewi nascitur anno tricesimo post discessum Patricii de Menevia. †
468 an. Quies Benigni episcopi.
  an. an. an. an. an. an.XXX an. an. an. an. an. an. an. an. an.
  an.XL an. an. an. an. an. an. an. an.L an. an. an. an. an. an.
501 an. Episcopus Ebur pausat in Christo anno CCCL aetatis suae.
  an. an. an.LX an. an. an. an. an. an. an. an. an. an. an.LXX an.
516 an. Bellum Badonis, in quo Arthur portavit crucem Domini nostri Jhesu Christi tribus diebus et tribus noctibus in humeros suos et Brittones victores fuerunt.
  an. an. an. an.
521 an. Sanctus Columcille nascitur.
  Quies sanctae Brigidae.
  an. an. an.LXXX an. an. an. an. an. an. an. an. an. an.XC an. an.
537 an. Gueith Camlann in qua Arthur et Medraut corruerunt, et mortalitas in Brittannia et in Hibernia fuit.
  an. an. an. an. an.
544 an. C Dormitatio Ciarani.
  an. an.
547 an. Mortalitas magna in qua pausat Mailcun rex Genedotae. †Unde dicitur, 'Hir hun Wailgun en llis Ros'. Tunc fuit wallwelen.
  an. an. an. an. an. an. an.CX an. an. an.
558 an. Gabran filius Dungart moritur.
  an. an. an.
562 an. Columcille in Brittannia exiit.
  an. an.CXX an. an. an. an. an.
†565 an. Navigatio Gildae in Hybernia. †
†569 an.Synodus Victoriae apud Brittones congragatur. †
570 an. Gildas †Britonus sapientissimus† obiit.
  an. an.
573 an. Bellum Armterid [inter filios Elifer et Guendoleu filium Keidiau; in quo bello Guendoleu cecidit; Merlinus insanus effectus est] .

574 an. CXXX Brendan Byror dormitatio.
an. an. an. an. an.
580 an. Guurci et Peretur [filii Elifer] moritur.
an. an. an. an.
584 an. CXL Bellum contra Euboniam et depositio Danielis Bancorum.
an. an. an. an.
589 Conversio Constantini ad Dominum.
an. an. an. an. an.CL
†594 an. Edilbertus in Anglia rexit.†
595 an. Columcille moritur.
Dunaut [filius Pabo] rex moritur.
Augustinus Mellitus Anglos ad Christum convertit.
an. an. an. an. an.
601 an. Sinodus Urbis Legion.
Gregorius obiit in Christo.
David episcopus Moni Judaeorum.
an. an. an.CLX an.
606 an. Depositio Cinauc episcopi.
607 an. Aidan map Gabran moritur.
an. an. an. an. an.
612 an. Conthigirni obitus et Dibric episcopi.
613 an. Gueith Cair Legion, et ibi cecidit Selim filii Cinan.
Et Jacob filii Beli dormitatio.
an.CLXX an.
616 an. Ceretic obiit.
617 an. Etguin incipit regnare.
an. an. an. an. an. an.
624 an. CLXXX Sol obscuratus est.
an.
626 an. Etguin baptizatus est, et Run filius Urbgen baptizavit eum.
627 an. Belin moritur.
an.
629 an. Obsessio Catguollaun regis in insula Glannauc.
630 an. Guidgar venit et non redit.
Kalendis januariis Gueith Meicen; et ibi interfectus est Etguin cum
duobus filiis suis; Catguollaun autem victor fuit.
631 an. Bellum Cantscaul in quo Catguollaun corruit.
632 an. Strages Sabrinae et jugulatio Iudris.
an. an.CXC an. an. an. an. an. an. an. an. an.
644 an. CC Bellum Cocboy in quo Oswald rex Nordorum et Eoba rex
Merciorum corruerunt.
645 an. Percussio Demeticae regionis, quando coenobium David
incensum est.
an. an. an. an.

†649 an. Guentis strages.†
650 an. Ortus stellae.
    an. an. an.CCX an.
656 an. Strages Gaii campi.
657 an. Pantha occisio.
658 an. Osguid venit et praedam duxit.
    an. an.
661 an. Commene fota.
662 an. Brocmail †Escithrauc† moritur.
    an. CCXX.
665 an. Primum Pasca apud Saxones celebratur.
    Bellum Badonis secundo.
    Morcant moritur.
    an. an. an.
669 an. Osguid rex Saxonum moritur.
    an. an. an. an. an. an.CCXXX an.
676 an. Stella mirae magnitudinis visa est per totum mundum lucens.
    an. an. an. an. an.
682 an. Mortalitas magna fuit in Brittannia, in qua Catgualart filius
    Catguolaun obiit.
683 an. Mortalitas †fuit† in Hibernia.
684 an. CCXL Terrae motus in Eubonia factus est magnus.
    an. an. an. an.
689 an. Pluvia sanguinea facta est in Brittannia, et †in Hyberniat† lac et
    butirum versa sunt in sanguinem.
    an. an. an. an. an.CCL an. an. an. an. an. an. an. an. an. an.
704 an. CCLX Alchfrit rex Saxonum obiit.
    Dormitatio Adomnan.
    an. an. an. an. an. an. an. an. an.
714 an. CCLXX Nox lucida fuit sicut dies.
    Pipinus major, rex Francorum, obiit in Christo.
    an. an.
717 an. Osbrit rex Saxonum moritur
718 an. Consecratio Michaelis archangeli †in monte Garganot† ecclesiae.
    an. an.
721 Aestas torrida.
722 an. Beli filius Elfin moritur. Et bellum Hehil apud Cornuenses, Gueith
    Gartmailauc, Cat Pencon, apud dexterales Brittones, et Brittones
    victores fuerunt in istis tribus bellis.
    an. an.CCLXXX an. an. an.
728 an. Bellum montis Carno.
    an. an. an. an. an. an. an.CCXC
735 Beda presbiter dormit.

736 Ougen rex Pictorum obiit.
an. an. an. an. an. an. an. an.CCC an. an. an. an. an.
750 an. Bellum inter Pictos et Brittones, id est Gueith Mocetauc. Et rex eorum Talargan a Brittonibus occiditur.
Teudubr filius Beli moritur.
an. an. an.
754 an. CCX Rotri, rex Brittonum, moritur.
an. an.
757 an. Ethwald rex Saxonum moritur.
an. an.
760 an. Bellum inter Brittones et Saxones, id est Gueith Hirford, et Dunnagual filius Teudubr moritur.
an. an. an. an.CCCXX an. an. an.
768 an. Pasca commutatur apud Brittones †super dominicam diem† emendante Elbodugo homine Dei.
an. an. an. an. an. an.CCCXXX
775 an. Fernmail filius Judhail moritur.
776 an. Cenioyd rex Pictorum obiit.
777 an. Cudberth abbas moritur.
778 an. Vastatio Brittonum dexteralium apud Offa.
an. an. an. an. an.
784 an. CCCXL Vastatio Brittonum cum Offa in aestate.
an. an. an. an. an. an. an. an. an. an. an.CCCL
796 an. †Vastatio Reinuch ab Offa† Primus adventus gentilium apud dexterales ad Hiberniam.
797 an. Offa rex Merciorum et Morgetiud rex Demetorum morte moriuntur, et bellum Rudglann.
an.
798 an. Caratauc rex Guenedotae apud Saxones jugulatur.
an. an. an. an. an. an.CCCLX an. an.
807 an. Arthgen rex Cereticiaun moritur. †Eclipsis solis.†
808 an. Regin rex Demetorum et Catell †rex† Povis moriuntur.
809 an. Elbodug archiepiscopus Guenedotae regione migravit ad Dominum.
810 an. †Luna obscuratur.† Combustio Miniu. †Mortalitas pecorum in Brittannia.†
811 an. Eugein filius Margetiud moritur.
812 an. Decantorum arx ictu fulminis comburit.
813 an.Bellum inter Higuel †et Kinan. Howel† victor fuit.
an.
814 an. CCCLXX Tonitruum magnum fuit et incendia multa fecit.
Trifun filius Regin moritur.
Et Griphiud filius Cincen dolosa dispensatione a fratre suo Elized post intervallum duorum mensium interficitur.

Higuel de Monia insula triumphavit et Cinan de ea expulit cum
contritione magna exercitus sui.
an.
816 an. Higuel de Monia expulsus est ††a Kenan.††
Cinan rex moritur.
†Saxones montes Ereri et regum Roweynauc invaserunt†.
817 an. Gueith Lannmaes.
an. an. an. an.
818 an. †Ceniul regiones Demetorum vastavit.†
an. an. an. an.
822 an. Arcem Decantorum a Saxonibus destruitur et regionem Poyvis
in sua potestate traxerunt.
an. an.CCCLXXX
825 an. Higuel moritur.
an. an. an. an. an.
831 an. †Eclipsis lunae.† Laudent moritur et Saturnbiu Hail Miniu moritur.
an. an. an.CCCXC an. an. an. an. an.
840 an. Nobis episcopus in Miniu regnavit.
an.
842 an. Iudguollaun moritur.
an.
844 an. CCCC Mermin moritur. Gueith Cetill.
an. an. an.
848 an. Gueit Finnant. Judhail rex Guent a viris Broceniauc occisus est.
849 an. Mouric occisus est a Saxonibus.
850 an. Cinnen a gentilibus jugulatur.
an. an.
853 an. Mon †est† vastata a gentilibus nigris.
854 an. CCCCX Cinnen rex Povis in Roma obiit.
an.
856 an. Cenioyth rex Pictorum moritur. Et Jonathan princeps Opergelei
moritur.
an. an. an. an. an.
860 an. †Mail Eachlen obiit.†
862 an. Catgueithen expulsus est.
an.
864 an. CCCCXX Duta vastavit Gliuisigng.
865 an. Cian Nant Nimer obiit.
866 an. Urbs Ebrauc vastata est, id est Cat Dub Gint.
an. an.
869 an. Cat Brin Onnen.
870 an. Arx Alt Clut a gentilibus fracta est.
871 an. Guoccaun mersus est, rex Cereticiaun.
an.

873 an. Nobis †episcopus† et Mouric moriuntur. Gueith Bannguolou.
an.CCCCXXX
874 an. †Llunwerth episcopus consecratur.†
875 an. Dungarth rex Cerniu, †id est Cornubiae,† mersus est.
876 an. Gueith Diu Sul in Mon.
877 an. Rotri et filius ejus Guriat a Saxonibus jugulatur.
878 an. Aed map Neill moritur.
an.
880 an. Gueit Conguoy. Digal Rotri a Deo. †Gueit Conani.†
an.
882 an. Catgueithen obiit.
an. an. CCCXL
885 an. Higuel in Roma defunctus est.
887 an. Cerball defunctus est.
889 an. †Subin Scottorum sapientissimus obiit.†
892 an. Himeyd moritur.
894 an. CCCCL Anaraut cum Anglis venit vastare Cereticiaun et Strat Tiui.
895 an. Nordmani venerunt et vastaverunt Loycr et Bricheniauc et Guent
et Guinnliguiauc.
an. an. an. an.
896 an. †Panis in Hibernia defecit. Vermes de aere ceciderunt talpae
similes cum duobus dentibus qui totam comederunt; qui ejecti
ṣunt jejunio et oratione.†
898 an. †Elstan rex Saxonum obiit.†
900 an. Albrit rex Giuoys moritur.
an.
902 an. Igmunt in insula Mon venit et tenuit Maes Osmeliaun.
903 an. †Merwyn filius Rodri obiit et† Loumarch filius Himeid moritur.
904 an. CCCCLX Rostri †filius Heweid† decollatus est in Arguistli.
an.
906 an. Gueith Dinmeir et Miniu fracta est.
907 an. Guorchiguil †episcopus† moritur †et Cormuc rex.†
908 an. Asser †episcopus† defunctus est.
909 an. Catell †filius Rodri† rex moritur.
an. an. an.
913 an. Otter venit †in Britanniam.†
an. CCCCLX
915 an. Anaraut rex †Britonum† moritur.
an.
917 an. Aelfled regina obiit.
an.
919 an. Clitauc rex occisus est.
an.

921 an. Gueith Dinas Neguid.
     an. an. an.CCCCLXXX an. an. an.
928 an. Higuel rex perrexit ad Romam. †Helena obiit.†
     an. an. an. an. an. an.CCCCXC an. an. an.
935 an. †Grifinus filius Oweyn obiit.†
938 an. Bellum Brune.
939 an. Himeid filius Clitauc et Mouric moritur.
941 an. Aedelstan †rex Saxonum† moritur.
     an.
942 an. Abloyc rex moritur.
943 an. Catel filius Artmail veneno moritur.
     Et Iudgual †filius Rodri† et filius ejus Elized a Saxonibus
     occiduntur.
944 an. D Lunberth episcopus in Miniu obiit.
     an.
945 an. †Morleis episcopus obiit.†
946 an. Cincenn filius Elized veneno periit.
     Et Eneuris episcopus Miniu obiit.
     Et Strat Clut vastata est a Saxonibus.
947 an. Eadmund rex Saxonum jugulatus est.
     an. an.
950 an. Higuel rex Brittonum †scilicet Bonus† obiit.
951 an. Et Catguocaun filius Ovein a Saxonibus jugulatur.
     Et bellum Carno †inter filios Hoeli et filios Idwal.†
     an. an.
952 an. †Iago et Idwal filii Idwal vastaverunt Dewet.†
954 an. DX Rotri, filius Higuel, moritor.
     an. an. an. an. an. an. an. an. an. an.DXX an. an. an. an. an. an. an. an.
     an. an.DXXX an. an. an.

INDEX OF PROPER NAMES

References are to chapter numbers followed by the year in the Welsh Annals, prefixed A.

Bassas, 56
Bavarians, 17
Bavarus, 17
Bearnoch, 57
Bebba, 63
Bede, A735
Beli, son of Elffin, A722
Belin, A627
Belinus, 19
Benignus, A468
Benlli, 32
Beornec, 57
Bernicia, 56, 61, 63
Bernicians, 57, 61
Beulan, 10
Bluchbard, 61
Boib, 17
Bolg, 14
Bonus, 49
Bowness, 27
Brand, 61
Brendan of Birr, A574
Briacat, 49
Bridei, 57
Brigit, 16, A494, 521
Britain, British, Britons, *passim*
Britto, 10, 11
Britto, son of Hessitio, 17
Brocmail, A662
Brunanburgh see Brune, battle of
Brune, battle of, A938
Brutus, 7, 10, 15, 17, 18
Brycheiniog, A848, 895
Brynonnen, A869
Builth, 48, 49, 73
Burgundians, 17
Burgundus, 17

Cabal, 73
Cadafael, 65
Cadell, 35, A808
Cadell, son of Rhodri, A909
Cadell, son of Arthfael, A943
Cadwaladr, 64, A682

Cadwallon, 61, 64, A629, 630,
    631, 682
Cadwgan, son of Owain, A951
Caergloiu, see Gloucester
Caergwrtheyrn, 42
Caer Pentaloch, 23
Caer Seint, 25
Cafal, see Cabal
Cainan, 17
Camlann, battle of, A537
Cantscaul, 64, A631
Canturguoralen, see Kent
Capen, 10
Cappadocians, 18
Caradog, A798
Carausius, 23, 24
Cardigan, see Ceredigion
Carno, A728, 951
Carrow, river, 23
Casser, 59
Cateyrn, 44, 48
Catgueithen, A862, 882
Catwallaun, see Cadwallon
Celestine, Pope, 50, 51
Celyddon, 56
Cenail, 23
Cenwulf, A818
Cerball, A887
Ceredig, A616
Ceredigion, 74, A807, 871, 894
Ceretic, 37, 63
Ceris, whirlpool of, 75
Cernyw, A875
Cetill, battle of, A844
Chester, A601, 613
Cian, 62
Cian of Nanthyfer, A865
Ciaran, A544
Cinaed, see Kenneth
Citheinn, vale of 75
Cities, of Britain, list of, 66a
Claudius, 21
Clyde, 28
Clydog, A919, 939

94

Enoch, 17
Enos, 17
Eobba, 56, 57, 61
Eomer, 60
Eormenric, 58
Episford, 44
Equitius, 31
Erconbert, 58
Erectonius, 10
Eryri, see Snowdon
Essex, 46
Ethach, 17
Ethel, see Aethel
Eubonia, see Man, isle of
Eucharistus, 22
Ezra, 17

Felix, 66
Fetebir, 17
Ffernfeal, 49, A775
Ffinant, A848
Finn, 31
Folcwald, 31
Francus, 17
Franks, 17, A714
Frealaf, 31
Fredulf, 31
Freodwald, 63
Fufius, 66

Gabrán, son of Dungart, A558,
   607
Gaius Field, battle of, 64, A656
Garan, 57
Gargano, A718
Garth Maelog, battle of, A722
Gaul, 10, 18, 27, 28
Gechbrond, 57
Gepids, 17
Gepidus, 17
Germany, 31, 43, 56
Geta, 31
Gewissi, A900
Gildas, A565, 570

Glannauc, A629
Glein, river, 56
Gloiu, 49
Gloucester, 49
Glywysing, 41, A864
Gomer, 18
Gorchymyl, A907
Gorheli, springs of, 70
Goths, 17, 18
Gothus, 17
Gower, 14, 71
Gratian, 27, 29, 31
Greece, 10
Greeks, 18
Gregory, 63, A601
Gruffydd, son of Cyngen, A814
Gruffydd, son of Owain, A935
Guaul, 23, 38
Guinnion, 56
Gwallawg, 63
Gwenddolau, son of Ceidio, A573
Gwent, 70, 72, A649, 848, 895
Gwerthrynion, 47, 48, 49
Gwgon, A871
Gwrgi, A580
Gwriad, A877
Gwyddgant, 49
Gwyddgar, A630
Gwynedd, 40, 61, 62, 64, 65, A798,
   809
Gwynessi, 42
Gwynllywiog, A895
Gwyrangon, 37

Ham, race of, 10, 17
Hehil, battle of, A722
Helen, A928
Hengest, 31, 37, 38, 43, 45, 46, 56
   58
Hereford, A760
Hesitio, 17, 18
Horsa, 31, 38, 43, 44
Hryp, 59
Humber, 61

98

Penquaul, 23
Pepin II, A714
Peredur, A580
Picts, 7, 8, 12, 15, 23, 27, 30, 31,
  36, 38, 50, 57, 65, 67, A736,
  750, 776, 856
Postumus, 11
Powys, 35, A808, 822, 854
Priam, 10
Pybba, 60, 65
Pydew Meurig, 72

Quentouic, 27

Renchidus, 63
Rhain, A808, 814
Rhea, 17
Rheinwg, son of Offa, A796
Rhodri, A754, 877, 880, 903
Rhodri, son of Hyfaidd, A904
Rhodri, son of Hywel, A954
Rhuddlan, A797
Rhufoniog, A816
Rhun, son of Urien, pref, 57, 63,
  A626
Rhyd yr Afael, see Episford
Rhydderch Hen, 63
Rieinmellt, 57
Riez, 48
Romans, 10, 15, 19, 20, 27, 28,
  30, 31
Romanus, 17
Rome, 50
Rothmund, 59
Rowenna, 37
Royth, 57
Rubellius, 66
Rufus, 66

St. Faustus, 48
St. Germanus, 32, 33, 34, 35, 39,
  44, 47, 48, 50, 51
St. Martin, 26, 28
St. Paulinus, 63

Sadyrnfyw, A831
Saebald, 61
Saefugl, 61
Samuel, 10
Saxo, 17
Saxons, 7, 16, 17, 31, A665, 704,
  717, 757, 760, 798, 816, 822,
  849, 877, 898, 941, 943, 946,
  947, 951
Scotia, 15
Scots, 15
Scythia, 15
Scythians, 15, 18
Segitius, 51
Sem, 17
Seth, 17
Severn, river, 9, 49, 68, 69, 72,
  A632
Severus, 23, 24
Severus II, 27
Sigegar, 61
Sigegeat, 61
Silvius, 11
Simeon, 17
Snowdon, 40, A816
Soemic, 61
Sogethere, 57
Sogor, 57
Spain, 13, 15
Stilicho, 66
Strathclyde, A946
Suibne, A889
Sussex, 46
Swaerta, 61
Swebdaeg, 61

Talhaearn, 62
Taliesin, 62
Talorgan, A750
Taurus, 66
Teifi, river, 47
Tewdwr, 49
Tewdwr, son of Beli, A750, 760
Thames, 9, 19, 20

99

100